First Year University Survival Guide
From Stress to Success

David Wang

Printed in the United States of America

First Printing, July, 2014

ISBN 978-0-9938133-0-6

David Wang
80 Arthur St. S
Elmira, ON, Canada, N3B2N4

Ordering information:
Go to www.imaprof.com or email
profdavidwang@gmail.com

Dedicated to my wonderful family

Acknowledgements

I would like to first, and foremost, thank my wife, Jodie, and children (Yo, Yi, Maggie, Maddie, Michelle, John, James, Monica and Jordan) for putting up with my antics and for being the wonderful individuals that they are, making every day an adventure. There is truly never a dull or quiet moment at the Wang household. I would like to thank my dad and my mom for raising me in the way that they did. Thanks go to my brother Michael and his family as well for their support over the years.

I would like to express my gratitude as well to my friends from Critical Mass over the years, the Handshake crew, all my soccer mates and my colleagues at the University of Waterloo.

To all my graduate students that I have supervised over the years, trust me when I say I have learned as much from you as you have from me.I greatly appreciate all the undergraduates that I have had the pleasure to teach.

To all my good friends, especially the Rosary group, who have supported me over the years, your love and prayers will never be forgotten.

Finally, I give my ultimate thanks to my God. Without Him and His good gifts, I would be nothing.

1. Introduction 1

2. Formula Sheet for Success 6

3. An Education System Gone Wrong 12

4. Keep Your Setbacks in Perspective 29

5. You Get Stronger One Mistake at a Time 36

6. Pain is Weakness Leaving the Body 41

7. Develop Grit 48

8. Reinvent Yourself 60

9. Strategize to Win the Game 65

   9.1 General Strategies 65

   9.1.1 Attitude toward Learning 65

     9.1.2 Deep Learning 67

   9.2 Specific Strategies 68

     9.2.1 Fundamentals 68

     9.2.2 Learning Styles 69

     9.2.3 Learn To Be a Serious Student 72

     9.2.4 Learn how to Read 74

     9.2.5 Learn how to Write 75

     9.2.5 Learn how to Speak 76

     9.2.6 Exam Preparation 78

     9.2.7 Time Management 80

9.2.8 Group Work 83

9.3 Cheating...84

10. Time is on Your Side 86

11. Keeping Balanced...88

12 Concluding Remarks...94

Bibliography 101

1. Introduction

In my conversations with other professors, a recent trend seems to be emerging. In universities everywhere, the ability of students to succeed and persevere in their studies is in jeopardy. Failures seem to be on the rise and there appears to be many causes. One could dwell on the causes but this is not the primary purpose of my writing this book. Because academia cannot afford to lower its standards, then the students themselves must somehow find a way to overcome the obstacles that are causing them to do poorly.

If you are reading this book, you may be a student who has just run into problems in your undergraduate studies or who is anxious about entering university and not being successful. Perhaps you have just failed a few midterms or perhaps you are just feeling overwhelmed about the amount of work that you need to go through. If so, this book is set up to try to help you through these difficulties. I have written this book in a slightly different format than you would normally expect from a book. Chapter 2 is a formula sheet with some helpful suggestions and hints to give you tools and perhaps a different perspective to immediately make changes to address your problems. Each suggestion on the formula sheet has an entire chapter attached to it that elaborates on how and why these hints will help you. I have tried to keep each chapter short and concise, with a few references attached so that you can explore in more detail, should you wish to do so. It is a different way to write a book, but I felt that this would be the most helpful way to organize my material efficiently.

Now, you are probably asking yourself why you should follow my advice. I am a professor of Electrical and Computer Engineering at the University of Waterloo, which is one of the top universities in Canada. It is well reputed for taking innovative approaches to learning and education, and takes pride in being the first university in Canada to introduce cooperative education (where students alternate terms between academic and work) directly into the curriculum. We have been called the "MIT of the North" and we do attract some of the best students in Canada. That being said, we are noticing a disturbing increase in the number of students who are failing or struggling in university.

I have been a professor for 25 years, starting when I was age 27. I have been recognized as a distinguished teacher but also have a good publication record in terms of scholarly activity. I care deeply about my students and not just in terms of their academics. I believe the worth of each person is more than just their course averages. My hope is that I can draw on my experiences mentoring over fifty graduate students, supervising design projects for nearly five hundred undergraduates and lecturing to thousands of students in order to give you some tools to help you achieve academic success.

I have also a great deal of expertise that I can draw from other areas of my life to provide valuable tools to help students. First, I have been an entrepreneur. A company that I co-founded in 2001, called Handshake Interactive Technologies Inc., was quite successful and was recognized as one of "Top 25 Up and Comer" technology companies in Canada by the Branham Group. I helped raise $3 million in Venture Capital financing in 2004. I then resigned as President of the company and returned to the university. During my tenure as president, the team that I had assembled had to face bankruptcy on several different occasions. Facing financial ruin and overcoming these obstacles was a huge learning experience and taught me how to persevere against what appeared at the time to be unsurmountable odds.

Another activity that I have been engaged in over the past two decades is the music industry. I am the founder, lead singer and lyricist of the band Critical Mass, which has won two Canadian Gospel Music Association awards for best Rock album (2000, 2005). We had the privilege to perform for over a million people at World Youth Day 2002 in Toronto, in one of the biggest gatherings of its kind ever in North America. I was also a music columnist for the Catholic Register in Canada for almost 15 years and helped to mentor numerous musical acts over the years. Given this track record, you may think that I am some sort of musical expert but the truth is that there are many other artists that are far more talented than I am. However, I have been persistent, used my network of contacts and acknowledged my limitations in order to ultimately achieve success far beyond what I had ever expected. Again, there are lessons here that I believe can be transferred into helping struggling students.

I have also been heavily involved in amateur sports. I have coached soccer for almost three decades. I have a passion for working with youth and drawing the best out of them. My most satisfying moments as a coach have not been winning championships (although one of my teams did win a provincial championship); rather, they are in seeing players developing a lifelong love of sports and exceeding what they thought possible simply through hard work and adjusting their mental attitude.

As well, I would be remiss not to mention that I have a beautiful family with 9 children (see Figure 1). They have succeeded in academics, sports and the arts. This did not come without a lot of struggles. There is no user manual for how to raise a large family and, at one time, our struggles almost tore our family apart. I had to make enormous adjustments in my lifestyle in order to save the most important treasure I have on this earth. I believe I am living proof that it is possible to radically change one's own behaviour when times are desperate.

Figure 1

Because of these varied life experiences, I hope that I can bring some of the lessons that I have learned to students who are struggling with their academics. I should mention that the focus of what follows is probably more relevant to Canadian universities and some of it is more relevant to engineering than other disciplines. However, I am confident that the main principles described in this book can be applied anywhere.

2. Formula Sheet for Success

I know that some of you may feel overwhelmed at the prospect of having to read an entire book in order to redeem your university studies, particularly since one factor leading to your troubles is that you haven't had the focus to read and time-manage in the first place. I decided to give you this chapter as a quick study guide to help you alter your study habits in a short period of time. Each of the topics below have an entire chapter devoted to the topic later in the book, so once you understand where your weaknesses are, you can always read in more detail.

1.   **Keep Your Setbacks in Perspective**

When students do poorly in a series of midterms, or an important project, it can create an overwhelming feeling of helplessness. If you are angry and blame an unfair exam or poor professor, it doesn't change the reality of your situation. If you feel totally hopeless and give up, then you have already lost the battle. It is important at this point to keep everything in perspective. What seems like a disaster now will, in the long term, seem trivial. In Chapter 4, you will see that even if you get fail and get 20% on all your midterms in a particular term, the impact on your overall final undergraduate average is miniscule. Look at this setback as an opportunity to learn and to modify your approaches to school, and be thankful that the damage is actually inconsequential. You need to put this behind you as quickly as possible, and focus on the future rather than dwelling on something that you can't change. After all, once you have graduated and are competing for jobs, you will find that your undergraduate averages are actually not important at all. It is more your job experiences and your network of friends that will be the most useful to you.

2.   You Get Stronger One Mistake at a Time

In my experience, people learn more from making mistakes than those who have never experienced failure or hardships. Most successful individuals that I have crossed paths with have had experienced devastating setbacks at some point in their lives. The difference between these individuals and those who have very run-of-the-mill careers is often how they respond to these obstacles. Those who look at mistakes as an opportunity to learn and grow are those who will ultimately be the most successful in whatever tasks they are tackling. Mistakes are actually an opportunity to flourish!

3.   Pain is Weakness Leaving the Body

At this point, you probably feel emotionally and perhaps even physically drained. There is a saying attributed to General Lewis B. Puller that "Pain is weakness leaving the body". Anything worth doing is going to involve sacrifice and dedication. *If it were easy, then everyone would be doing it.* You had the marks to get into your university program and, yes, you are hitting adversity. Just like an Olympic athlete, you now need to turn this pain into strength. Know that you are not alone but if you are willing to make the sacrifices and change how you work, you can succeed where others have failed. You may feel it is easier said than done, but every successful individual has hit the point where they decide that they are going to persevere, regardless of the sacrifice and the short term pain. The short-term pain is what will ultimately give you long-term gain.

4. **Develop Grit**

Related to the previous points is the concept of grit. In the past 5 years, there has been research that Intelligent Quotient (IQ), Emotional Quotient (EQ), SAT scores and most other standard indicators of academic ability have paled in comparison to a characteristic called "grit". This is essentially the ability to persevere in the presence of obstacles. There are grit scale tests and they are highly correlated to how successful students are in their studies. For example, the success of candidates in an undergraduate psychology program was shown to be highly correlated to grit. Even success in National Spelling Bees and the retention in the prestigious Westpoint Military Academy Boot Camp is highly correlated to grit. If you are a person that likes to change tasks often, then this could be a root cause of your problems. In this chapter, we will explore the concept of grit and some tools to help you develop aspects of this characteristic to help you achieve academic success.

5. **Reinvent Yourself**

This is critical to your success. When you experience failure, the tendency is often to blame external circumstances; poor assignments, unfair exams, incompetent professors, or not feeling well. However, these are all things that are out of your control. The only control you have is over yourself.

Recognizing that any chance of success must come from changes within yourself is the first step to reducing your academic difficulty. This is challenging because most of you have been, because of society's emphasis on boosting self-esteem, not prepared to look for faults in yourself. What is also difficult here is that you may need to change the people you associate with. You need to surround yourself with like-minded individuals who are dedicating themselves to academic success.

6. **Strategize to Win the Game**

Once you have dealt with the first five points, then it is time to start to modify how you study and "play the game". This chapter is the longest and will give you the most practical advice on how to succeed academically. It will require all the previous newly learned characteristics, as you will now have to religiously attend lectures, put away all distractions in class (e.g. laptops and Facebook) and totally relearn how to study. You need to focus on the aspects of the course that give the biggest payoffs. Don't spend dozens of hours on reports or labs that are worth few marks in the end. These tips given may not work for everyone as there are different learning modalities for different individuals. However, the ideas can be adapted to any student and the tips I have given are very general in nature.

7. **Time is on Your Side**

Hopefully, by implementing these changes, you can start to

improve your academic standing. Here, slow and steady truly does win the race. If you are just recovering from failures, make your goals reasonable. You may feel pressure to do more but it is not realistic. Keep your goals modest but strive diligently to meet them. Keep in mind that, for many people looking to hire, they are looking for upward trends in marks. In fact, if you have a bad term but manage to creep up every term with improving marks, you may be viewed as a better potential candidate than someone who has maintained the same average every year. Because you are improving every term, there is a chance you will continue this upward trend even after you have graduated! Remember, it is the trend that is almost as important as the final average!

8.   **Keep Balanced**

Unless you are one of the few people who can work 24/7, you will hit a point of diminishing returns. Most individuals work better with regular breaks, to get their mind on something different, if even for a few minutes every hour or a few hours every day. I am a big advocate of "healthy mind, healthy body". If you can get some exercise at the same time as you are taking a break, I suspect that you will find that you will be even more effective than you would be if you continued on a continuous study cycle. As well, it is good to do something spiritual for yourself. Reconnect yourself to something that is above and beyond your current circumstances. If you don't have any spiritual belief, then reach out to your community and do some charity work. Finally, try to find activities where you need to interact with other individuals beyond your current social circle. One of the realities is that successful people tend to have a large network of successful people to interact with. Currently, my soccer team, for example, is full of successful individuals who are a great source of help and connections. You really need to give yourself a bigger picture of life so that you can keep all your daily struggles in perspective.

Now, these eight points aren't a magical formula that, if you read, will help you pass. It means that you have to dedicate yourself to making some radical and difficult changes in your life. As well, these are points that I have uncovered in my research and in my life experiences. Every individual ultimately has to find a system that works for them. Consider this as just a starter-guide. You may find that not all these points are helpful but perhaps just a couple relate to your present situation. If so, use those as a starting point and remember that most of the great battles were won with the divide-and-conquer approach. Making many small improvements can add up to something significant.

3. An Education System Gone Wrong

Society has truly changed over the past few decades. We have gone from post-secondary education being a pursuit of a minority of gifted individuals to an expected right of virtually all graduating high school students. For Canada, in 1920, there were approximately 23,000 students in universities. This burgeoned to 300,000 students in the 1970s and has exploded to over a million students currently (Cote & Allahar, 2007). This would be a very encouraging statistic if it were not for another disturbing trend.

A Canadian survey involving 2000 out of 15000 faculty members/librarians in the province of Ontario pointed out that their first year students were immature and lazy. Over half of those surveyed noted this problem had actually worsened in the period from 2006-2009 (Rushowy, 2009). James Cote, the author of *Ivory Tower Blues: A University System in Crisis* , points the finger at a lack of work ethic in university students and high schools that no longer demanded discipline and deadlines. Cote also points out in his book that societal distractions, such as computer games and social media, make conventional learning from books appear mundane. Even worse, high schools used to help identify, from the general student population, those individuals who would benefit from a university education. Now, high schools are pushing students through with insufficient preparation and inflated grades (Cote & Allahar, 2007). Universities are now facing an unprecedented crisis where society, the educational system and technological advances have made it increasingly difficult for the student to actually succeed when they enter into university.

Universities also have a responsibility to maintain academic standards. Because of this, students are receiving a rude shock back to reality. Half of all students will see their marks decline by a letter grade going from high school to university. Another quarter will see their marks drop by two letter grades or more. Only one quarter of these students will have their marks stay steady and a miniscule 2.5% will see their average increase (Jerema, 2010). These drops naturally cause an increase in failure rates, which hits particularly hard in first year. In Canada in 2005, about 16 percent of undergraduate students ended up dropping out, with 14 percent dropping out in first year. The surveys of those who drop out suggest that particular reasons include the inability to meet deadlines and poor study behaviours (CTV News, 2009). There are as many as 40% of first year students who report having problems with learning strategies and with self-regulation strategies (Bentein, Frenay, Verwaerde, Bourgeois, & Galand, 2003).

It has been my experience that the situation has worsened in the last decade. The top 10% of the students I am teaching are probably as good as the top tier of students from the past when I started teaching in the late 1980s. However, the other 90% of the students are, in my opinion, slowly dropping in their abilities. I have been noting that the usual normal distribution of marks, at least in my courses, is slowly become a bimodal distribution with two peaks; one for the top 10% with a consistently high average but with another peak for the lower 90%. This lower peak is gradually dropping down in average, with a resulting increase in failure rates.

Some of the readers of this book, particularly those in high school, may have come into first year university with the expectation that they were destined to be in that top 10% of the first year class. After all, they had done similarly well in high school. This is a belief that is a result of grade inflation in high schools that has created the illusion that high marks guarantee success (Tamburri, 2012) (Schwartz, 2013). In the 1980s, the average entering grade for Ontario universities was a mid-B. Now, despite the increase in the number of first year students, the entrance averages range from a low A to a high A at some institutions (Cote & Allahar, 2007). Obviously, this does not reflect the actual ability of the students in these courses.

It is because of grade inflation that a high mark in a course no longer implies mastery of that subject. Unfortunately, not mastering the basic fundamental concepts in high school is a death knell in university. For example, almost a quarter of incoming students fail, in their first year, the English Language Proficiency (ELPE) examination at Waterloo. This is a very simple test of writing ability where the students have an hour to write a simple short 4-5 paragraph essay on a generic topic. The focus of the marks is on the mechanics of writing, such as spelling and grammar. As long as the student avoids slang and the essay is coherent, the student should easily pass since very little is based on the actual content of the essay.

The lack of fundamentals is not only in English but is across all subjects. According to data from the National Center for Education Statistics in the United States, twenty percent of first years are in a position where they are taking remedial classes (Griesemer, 2013). In Canada, a study conducted by the Ontario Confederation of University Faculty Associations showed that 55% of professors and librarians felt that first year students were more poorly prepared for their program than those enrolled just three years earlier, resulting in the creation of remedial courses (Rushowy, 2009). These same professors reported "a decline in students' writing and numeric skills, an over-reliance on Internet resources, lower maturity levels and an expectation of success without the requisite effort" (CTV News, 2009). James Cote points out that, "The shame is that many should not have advanced as far as they did, or if we really want so many to get so far, we should radically alter the primary and secondary systems to fully educate each student to achieve mastery in the required disciplines" (Cote & Allahar, 2007).

It is my opinion that high schools offer insufficient courses that focus on the fundamentals, and the problem is worsening. In Ontario, calculus has been reduced to the point where differentiation is taught but integration is not. For those who are not mathematically inclined, this is akin to teaching someone to drive forward but never teaching him how to back up. There seems to me to be a reluctance to force the students to memorize even simple things like the spelling of words, because of auto-correct in their computers. There seems to be a perception that, since we have the Internet and can "Google" it quickly anyways, there is no need to memorize. Although too much rote memorization is not useful, one does need to have some simple facts committed to memory. Students are also not used to thinking about the numbers they are manipulating since they can simply grab a calculator to do even the simplest of computations. Because of this, I am finding that this current generation of students cannot estimate roughly what answer they should get and blindly trust in the numbers that show on their screen, even if the results are ludicrous. Finally, the Internet is slowly eroding the students' ability to think critically. There is a tendency for students to believe everything they find on the Internet, without going through the process of rigorously examining the reliability of the source of the information. All of these factors are contributing to the lack of fundamental tools that students bring into their university studies.

Informal surveys I have conducted in my own classes also indicate that first year students feel that their high schools have inadequately prepared them for the amount of work that they would encounter in university. The students also do not feel that the lax deadlines imposed in high school helped them to cope with the strict deadlines that they now have to meet in university. In fact, the vast majority feel that they have been greatly let down by their secondary schools.

I believe that part of the problem with student preparation may also be due to the lack of adequately trained teachers, particularly with respect to certain crucial subjects, such as Mathematics and English. My observation is that many of the generation of teachers who have graduated since the early 2000s are part of the wave of students who were taught using the whole language philosophy of the 1980s. This created a teaching paradigm where grammar, phonics and spelling were de-emphasized in favor of a more holistic approach. This was also the same time that schools began heavily incorporating computers and calculators in the early grades, instead of learning to do mathematical calculations by hand. Once these students became teachers, this became a problem of the blind leading the blind since we have a generation of teachers who may not have the background to teach the fundamentals in a rigorous fashion.

Another part of the problem is the substantial lack of cooperation between secondary and post-secondary institutions. The Bridge Project in the United States found that high schools are failing due in part to a lack of communication between their governing boards and those of the universities (Rigoglioso, 2005). A survey of educators opinions about how ready high schoolers were in 2012 stated that, "A large gap still exists between how high school teachers perceive the college readiness of high school graduates and how college instructors perceive the readiness of their incoming first-year students" (ACT, 2013). In fact, only a quarter of professors felt that incoming freshmen were well or very well prepared for first year even though 90 percent of high school teachers felt that way. Almost all of the high school teachers felt at least half the students were reading at appropriate grade level, but that does raise the alarming question about the preparation of the other half of the students. Until both high schools and universities begin to communicate and are able to assess student preparedness in the same manner, these trends are bound to continue.

To exacerbate the problem, students now entering into university have a poor work ethic. In my opinion, a bare minimum of time spent studying for a particular course in university is two hours for every hour of lectures. This implies that a university student should normally spend about six hours weekly on each course that has three hours of weekly lectures. If one has a five course workload in a term, that would mean approximately 30 hours of out-of-class study time in addition to the 15 hours of lecture. However, a survey conducted in the United States about how much senior high school students spend studying in their final year before university shows a huge disconnect with what they will need to do in university. In 2002, only a third of high school students spent more than six hours per week studying for *all* their courses. This was down from the 1980s where the ratio was closer to half of the students (Cote & Allahar, 2007). This is happening a time when marks continued to inflate in high school. Once in university, these students continue to think in terms of minimal effort. Another survey by the National Survey of Student Engagement indicates that 36 percent of university students in 2000 spent only 11 hours or less of out-of-class study time on all their academic activities. This is even more alarming when this same survey conducted only two years later indicated that this number rose to 44 percent (Cote & Allahar, 2007)! Is it any wonder that first year students often expect professors to spoon-feed and push them through with minimal individual effort? After all, this had been their high school experience.

Hand in hand with this lazy behaviour is a lack of ethics. When time runs out to complete their work, many students then resort to cheating. Almost two-thirds of students in high school claim that they have cheated on a test in their courses (Steinberg, Brown, & Dornbusch, 1997). This is an incredibly alarming statistic and this practice carries through to university. In 2011-2012, 7,000 undergraduate students were caught cheating in Canada but surveys indicate that more than 50 percent admit that they were guilty of academic dishonesty (Moore, 2014).

Perhaps one factor contributing to all these problems is a society-wide emphasis on creating self-esteem in our youth. Since the 1970s, psychologists have promulgated the theory that self-esteem is the key to happiness and success. Now we are seeing the fruits of this philosophy and there are researchers who are asking us to rethink this premise (Baumeister, 2005). In fact, studies now seem to indicate that high grades cause high self-esteem and not vice versa as was previously thought (Crocker & Park, 2004). When one tries to give students a false sense of self-esteem to try to improve student success, this is akin to putting the cart before the horse.

As a professor, I find that this sense of false self-esteem also leads to an attitude of self-entitlement. It is hard to teach students that you cannot criticize, even in a constructive manner. When an instructor does so in order to help the student, they can be attacked through course evaluations. It is not uncommon for students to come to me to ask for marks when they are not deserved. It is bewildering when the reason they ask for these marks is that they just need or want the higher mark. In my opinion, this has been fostered by the secondary school practice of passing students when they really should not have, in order to preserve their self-esteem.

To make matters worse, social media is amplifying this narcissistic attitude. As I am writing this in 2014, the dominant social media is Facebook, Twitter and Instagram, but the very nature of social media is that the dominant platform is always in flux. Regardless of which platform is currently dominating, the major goal of these social media is essentially to foster a "look at me" attitude. The youth of today are endlessly sending out notifications of where they are, whom they are with, whom they are following and taking "selfies" to display out to the world. This encourages the student to view the universe as revolving around themselves and their activities/interests. They no longer see themselves as part of a bigger machine where, if they don't do their part, they will be viewed as a failed component and discarded.

As part of the misguided attempt to promote self-esteem amongst our youth, even sports are having losers and winners taken out of the picture. Years ago, it seems that minor league sports would hand out medals to just the winners but in the 1980s, the practice began of handing out participation medals to everyone. Although this is, in itself, a harmless activity, there are now initiatives to accelerate the process of ensuring that there are no longer winners or losers. Although this is partially to ensure that kids never feel bad about themselves when participating in sports, things are being carried to extremes. In Canada, Sports Canada has started an initiative to eliminate competition in our youth (Canadian Sports Centres, 2005). In fact, the Ontario Soccer Association has decided, for youth under the age of 13, that there will no longer be scores recorded or standings kept. Tournaments are now referred to as "Festivals", to discourage the notion of a winner (Carlson, 2012). Things have gone so far that a soccer association in Ontario declared that a team that wins by more than five goals will forfeit their win (Friday, 2010). The net result of these changes is that we will soon have students entering university having *never* experienced losing or persevering over adversity as part of a team. The only window of opportunity for competition would be at the age of 13. After that, students enter secondary school, where most students opt out of team sports (except the clique referred to as jocks). For a university professor, the prospect of even more undergraduates who are woefully unprepared for the competitive and teamwork side of university studies is frightening.

The self-esteem problem is being made worse, as well, by a phenomenon referred to as helicopter parenting, where parents hover about their child's every activity to ensure that their little treasures will never have to suffer and get hurt. This current generation of youth have parents that plan every moment of their lives (Goodman, 2012). Parents are encouraged to be their child's friend and enrich their lives with endless stimulation and indulgences. When the child runs into difficulties, external causes are blamed rather than looking at the situation to see if the child is actually the responsible party. Where once a child would be chastised for poor academic performance, it is now more common practice to criticize the teachers. This leads to the ludicrous scenario, which is seen by more and more professors now, where parents are calling university administrators, deans and chairs to complain about how their child has been dealt with unfairly. They cannot believe that it is possible that their child is failing when they are investing so much money into their children's tuitions. It is hard to tell the parents that professors do not fail students… they fail themselves.

The helicopter parent mentality is evident everywhere I look. In Canada, we see more and more schools built with one-way driveways that have "kiss and drop" zones, where children are dropped off by their parental chauffeurs. I see fewer and fewer children walking to school anymore. When I speak to parents, this phenomenon is apparently driven by fear. I am told that the walk is not safe and the child could be accosted by a bully or a sexual predator. The net result of all this paranoia is that children no longer have an opportunity to learn to be independent. Some school administrators have even gone to the extreme of banning balls from the schoolyard because of the potential of injury (McMahon, 2011). While it was once common to explore the world on a bicycle, parents now feel the need to monitor their child's every moment, driving them back and forth to every activity. The result of this is a lack of experience in the real world. Children used to experience play with actual people and objects in the real world. In (Goodman, 2012), it is argued that, "The elementary years are for engaging children with natural phenomena, like gardens, animals and light. The child is expected to store such encounters in her memory and, from an accumulation of experiences, create and test her own concepts". This is gone when children are not allowed out to explore by helicopter parents.

When children do not have the opportunity to explore the real world, then they are then drawn to a virtual electronic world. Computers and all the other technology around a youth (e.g. game consoles, calculators, smartphones, tablets) are hindering the students' ability to cope once they enter university. It seems contradictory since many of these items, if used correctly, should help the students. Information that was once only found in libraries is now instantly accessible with a few keystrokes on the Internet. Word processing has made writing and editing simple, along with tools like spell check. One rarely needs a pen and paper for mathematics since the ease of calculators and spreadsheets is faster and more accurate. These devices however, have all instead stunted the ability for students to grow and learn. In the past, students were encouraged to write essays carefully, providing careful outlines and critical thinking. Papers were methodically researched and cited. Now, many students just open up their laptops and begin typing quickly, relying on auto-correct, which results in totally incoherent and disorganized drivel. Information is copied right off the Internet without checking the reliability of the source. Students are often unable to construct a coherent argument in written form. With calculators, students frequently cannot even do simple computations in their head and have no sense of when their calculators give them answers which are wrong by orders of magnitude.

The education system is introducing computers far too early in a child's education. In Canada, schools have a million computers which is a 5:1 student to computer ratio. Yet, the research is showing that the use of computers has an adverse effect on learning. It appears that greater access to computers and the Internet leads to lowest test scores, once all other factors such as household income are accounted for (Ferguson, 2005). Computers are great if they are truly used for educational purposes but most of time, they are being used for games, surfing and chatting.

The issues with computer technology and games go beyond just their misuse in education. For the typical youth now, amusement has switched from playing football to using your fingers and thumbs to interact in a virtual computer-generated world. The average child will spend 2000 hours yearly at the keyboard by age 10 (Collins, 2011). There is evidence that this much computer use causes students to be anti-social as this activity can doesn't stimulate the child's entire brain and can impair development (Matthews, 2001).

To make matters worse, hour long television shows have been replaced by three minute YouTube videos, needing far less attention span but needing extreme entertainment value in order to go viral. There are even some websites, like Vine, that reduce this to a mind-numbing 6 seconds. Reading is quickly becoming a lost art, where often the last book that most teens have read is Facebook. All this is contributing to a deterioration of the attention span that students need in order to succeed in school and in life.

The ability to communicate has also degraded because of technology. Written communication between individuals has switched from eloquent letters and phone calls to emails and now to terse text messages of only 140 characters. Expediency, rather than accuracy and coherent thought, is now valued. It is difficult to convince students that "txting is not 4 u". In fact, I often get emails with such shorthand in it.

Although students, parents and teachers all have role to play in the current situation, the universities are also hampered in their ability to create a solution to this problem due to resource limitations. Professors are now facing three times as many students as generation ago (Cote & Allahar, 2007). They now need to spend more time weeding out students that used to be screened out in high school. Students are now referred to by university administrators as clients or customers. This is a terrible change in focus. Because they are customers, the students expect grades and academic success in exchange for tuition.

Higher tuitions are now being charged due to government cutbacks. This has had another effect. More students are needing to work in order to pay for their education. This increases the likelihood that these students will struggle to complete their program. Balancing a full time job and being a full time student is not conducive to academic success.

There are some that will argue that universities are also beginning to lower their standards. In Ontario, funding is not only tied to the number of students enrolled but is also to retention. A high failure rate will, at some point, result in reduced funding for a university. There is incredible pressure to increase retention rates. One consequence of this is a decrease in the difficulties of the courses to address declining student abilities. For example, in most of my courses, if I were to give an exam that I gave twenty years ago to students now, there would likely be a sudden and drastic increase in failure rates. Even though I have tried to resist lowering my standards, when I look back over the past two decades at the difficulty of my courses and the amount of content delivered in a typical semester, I would have to admit that I have let things slide. That being said, as universities realize that standards can no longer be compromised, then we will again have failure rates rising.

Personally, I have found that my fellow professors are very stressed and many are no longer enjoying their job, particularly when it comes to the teaching component. Almost every professor can give a horror story about an unprepared and self-entitled student. In my case, I had a lazy student discover the night before a final exam that he was running out of time and did not want to study the last section of the course. Instead of working harder, this student looked at the course syllabus, discovered some unclear language regarding the last section of the course being on the final exam, and emailed me to threaten to launch an academic challenge if any material from the last section appeared on the final exam. It was also clear that this student had not come to the last two weeks of lectures, as it was emphasized in every class that this material would be on the final exam. In the end, all the students were offered an option to take the exam without the final section and to have their marks redistributed amongst the other questions. The amount of stress and planning to create a fair scenario for all made this teaching experience one of the worst I had ever experienced. All of this was because of the lack of work ethic of one student.

It appears that we are now at a crossroads with respect to post-secondary education. As mentioned, all the aforementioned societal changes (social media, the Internet, calculators and computers) have the potential to greatly enhance an individual's life. However, one effect of all these changes is the expectation of instant gratification. Patience and work ethic appears to be on the decline, and the very thought that suffering could be good for the soul would make most of students absolutely shudder. This present generation of students has lived in a privileged bubble which is now bursting at the most inopportune time: in university. If you are reading this, it is quite possible that you are one of these casualties. The good news is that I have seen many students overcome their initial problems and go on to excel in university.

I hope that the following chapters will guide and inspire you to make changes so that you can be among those that can say that they were able to succeed and thrive in university.

4. Keep Your Setbacks in Perspective

I don't know the circumstances that have brought you to this book. Perhaps you are worried about upcoming exams or assignments. You may just have failed a midterm or final exam. Perhaps you just received a mark in a project that is devastatingly low compared to what you are used to getting in high school. For many students, this setback seems insurmountable. This chapter is to help you keep your difficulties in perspective.

In the previous chapter, I spoke about how schools, sports and helicopter parents have taken failure out of the equation for many youth. However, setbacks are the best way to learn and grow as an individual. More and more researchers and psychologists agree that, in our children, allowing them to stumble is the best way for kids to learn resilience (Boesveld, 2013). It is also the best way to learn about innovation as one can only truly do novel things if one is allowed to fail in the pathway to creating the truly unique. After all, one often hears that Thomas Edison failed 1,000 times before finally inventing the light bulb.

I can hear some of you complaining now, however, that you are in university and are no longer a child. You might feel that it is too late to bounce back. You may believe that this lesson about keeping setbacks in perspective has come a decade too late for you. Let me reassure you that this is not true. Some of my best graduate students have had to bounce back from disastrous starts in their first year to eventually complete a doctorate degree. The following information will hopefully help you put everything into perspective.

First, try not to blame external factors. "The prof was bad", "the exam was unfair" or "my group members were lazy" are excuses that I have heard countless times. I don't want to imply that these complaints are not legitimate. However, these are factors that are beyond your control. Focusing on these issues won't help you develop a strategy to ultimately do well in the course. The only thing that is within your control is YOU.

Some students feel that, by persistently complaining about these external factors with their professor, that they will eventually wear down the instructor and get what they want. In my opinion, this is a foolhardy tactic. By continually pestering the professor, you may create an adversarial scenario. You might get a few marks in the short term but it can serve to hurt your cause in the long run.

You may be skeptical that I can help you since, in Chapter 1, it seems that I have been involved in a lot of activities and have had success in several areas. However, life has not always kind. In 2009, we moved into a new house but we were still trying to sell our old house. We were mistakenly quoted the wrong type of insurance by our insurance broker and, when a pipe broke at the top floor in our old house, the entire interior of the house was destroyed. The insurance company took advantage of the broker's mistake and refused to honor our policy. The resulting financial loss contributed to us having to file for bankruptcy. To add insult to injury, almost exactly a year later, the construction company doing some major work at the university by my office neglected to reinsulate the ceiling of my top floor office before going on Christmas holidays. Simultaneously, the university turned down the heat in my building for the holidays. The pipes directly over my office froze and cracked. As soon as the temperature rose enough to thaw the pipes, they burst directly over my office. By the time the campus police arrived, there was a foot of water in my office. Everything was destroyed, including notes, computers and other expensive equipment (see Figure 2).

Figure 2

I spent the next two months salvaging what little was left of two decades of teaching and research. Although much was eventually replaced through insurance, it also meant that a lot of my activities had to be restarted from scratch. Even though my setbacks were all caused by external factors, all I could control was my response. There was no alternative but to dig deep and plan for the future.

My situation was not unique and neither is yours. There have been many others that have faced similar situations, particularly in school, to persevere. Albert Einstein was not admitted to Zurich Polytechnic School and was thought to be quite stupid and anti-social. Others that were similarly academically challenged included Winston Churchill and Charles Darwin. Society should count itself lucky that these individuals did not give up.

Sports are full of stories about those who have been told they weren't good enough and yet they persevered. My personal story involves a student who was one year younger than me at my own high school. His name is Brian Skrudland and he was a local star with our Junior A hockey team, the Saskatoon Blades. However, he was never drafted by any NHL team. That is the academic equivalent of being told to leave school for good and abandon your dream. Brian, however, continued to work hard and eventually worked his way up the ranks to play for the Montreal Canadiens in the NHL. He still has the record for the fastest overtime goal in Stanley Cup history. All of this from a player that no team initially wanted to even take a look at!

Given my love of music, I have always been inspired by musicians who have had setbacks and persevered. The best example is The Beatles, who were turned down by Decca records in their first critical audition. Not only were they turned down but were allegedly told that they had no future in show business. Despite this rejection, the band kept going and Decca is now famous for one of the biggest blunders ever made in the music business. At the time, however, the "Fab Four" must have been devastated to have been turned down by a major record label.

Most successful entrepreneurs have also faced difficulties. Henry Ford failed miserably before becoming the founder of Ford Motor Company. Bill Gates dropped out of Harvard and had his first business ventures all fail. Colonel Sanders didn't find success until he was 75, having failed hundreds of times. Steve Jobs left Apple after losing the confidence of his board of directors. Starting over again, he ended up founding Pixar Animation, which revolutionized the animation industry, before returning to triumphantly lead Apple's rise back to the top of the tech world.

If you have just experienced a setback for one of the first times in your life, keep in mind that you are following in the footsteps of many others who have ended up being hugely successful. Just as you can't put the blame on external forces, you also can't look at this one set of disappointments as defining your worth as a person. You are more than a set of marks and you must draw on inner strength to move on.

However, at this point, if you feel totally hopeless and give up, then you have already lost the battle. It is important to keep everything in perspective. What seems like a disaster now will, in the long term, seem trivial. In a sense, the good news is that the majority of those around you who are encountering stumbling blocks will give up. You simply need to rise above them at this point.

It is probably quite difficult at the moment to keep everything in perspective. You may be devastated, depressed and angry. You may feel that you are now facing insurmountable odds to try to catch up. However, let's go through some typical scenarios to demonstrate that all is not lost. Suppose you have failed one midterm badly in your first term at school. Let's assume you received 20% in a midterm that is worth thirty percent of your final mark. Now, suppose you don't give up and you end up with a 70% overall average after you graduate. As well, let's suppose you have 5 courses per term, 2 terms per year and four years to complete your degree. This midterm mark that you received is lower by 50% from your eventual average. So effectively, you have lost 70%-20%=50% of the total midterm marks for that course. Since the midterm was worth thirty percent of the final mark, your overall mark for that course is now down by 15% from your eventual average! Sounds pretty bad except this disastrous mark will be averaged out by the other 40 courses you have taken! Once you divide the 15% by 40, the final impact on your average is only .37%, which is really quite insignificant. Knowing this, this failure now does not seem so important in the long run.

Now, suppose the situation is even more dire and you have failed all your course midterms with marks of 20%. That is five courses and your overall term average in all those courses for the term will drop by 15%. However, you have 8 terms overall which means the impact on your final overall average is less than 2%. I can guarantee you that this is a small enough number that it will have absolutely no impact on your career path. This is why it makes no sense for students to give up after their first set of midterms. If you can modify your approach to school and can persevere, what seems devastating at this point will, in time, turn out to have a negligible effect on your life.

Look at this moment of your life as an opportunity to modify your approaches to learning. Be thankful that the damage is quite small. You need to put this behind you as quickly as possible, and focus on the future rather than dwelling on something that you can't change. After all, once you have graduated and are competing for jobs, you will find that your undergraduate averages are not as important as your job experiences and your network of contacts.

5. You Get Stronger One Mistake at a Time

I have been a soccer coach for over 30 years now. I have worked with kids of all ages and abilities, from house league to travel teams. One indoor soccer team I coached in my youth won a provincial championship in my home province of Saskatchewan. That team was a particularly satisfying experience in that, in a lot of ways, the players consisted of kids that other coaches felt were un-coachable. However, the team was able to come together and do some amazing things. The same year they won a provincial championship, they also won a men's third division championship. All of this was accomplished by a group of 16 year olds.

My philosophy when coaching sports has two main mantras. The second one will be the subject of the next chapter but the first one is "Our team gets better one mistake at a time." This is something I repeat to my players constantly. Although some coaches try to work with their players (or worse, yell at them) so that they are only allowed certain predefined and specific roles in order to minimize mistakes and maximize winning, I believe this creates little coach-controlled robots who really never fully understand the game. My teams are encouraged to be creative, continuing to use those ideas that work and discarding those that don't. I never yell at a player for making a mistake but may have a discussion with him about other options that may yield a better result. I believe that people learn best when they have made a mistake and then change their behavior on their own. If a player is afraid to ever make a mistake, then he never learns to work independently.

Now, if you have just done poorly on an exam or set of exams, hopefully the previous chapter has shown you that not all that much has been lost. In fact, I would argue that this impediment may actually be a blessing in disguise. Consider an army going into battle. The general has no idea of the strength or tactics of the enemy force. To assess his enemy, the general will often send out a reconnaissance mission. The job of this mission is to learn more about the enemy. If the enemy engages and even destroys the reconnaissance forces, important information can be sent back to the general to create an opportunity to win the war. When you do poorly on an exam, you actually have learned a great deal. You now have an idea of the professor's examination style. You also know that your approach for studying did not work and it is time to change tactics. In other words, you have gathered valuable intelligence about the enemy (in this case, unfortunately the analogy paints the professor as the villain). This information, if you choose to use it, will enable you to win the war at the end. In a future chapter, we will talk about some possible ways to change your learning strategies, but it could be as simple as trying to find some other old exams from the professor, and practice in a mock exam scenario.

In an interesting book entitled *Sometimes You Win- Sometimes You Learn* (Maxwell, 2013), the author, John Maxwell, focuses on how to learn from your failures and mistakes to persevere. He elucidates on strategies to turn losses from mistakes into a gain by learning from the mistakes. To do this, the author suggests that a person must first take personal responsibility for the mistake. Don't blame external factors. Think about what went wrong and try to make changes to create a different outcome. This may mean you may need to step out of your comfort zone. It also means accepting that these changes may have to be a continual chain of possibly small changes and not just a one-time thing. You should choose small enough changes so that you can gain confidence with each small victory. Remember that a mistake is just feedback to help you move forward.

The author also encourages one to choose to hope. It must be a conscious decision. Visualize success and picture the steps you need to get there. If you lose hope, then you have essentially lost everything. Almost as important, however, is a humble and teachable spirit. If you don't believe that you have made a mistake and must learn from it, then you will be like the soccer player who refuses to pass, stubbornly believing that he is too good and can defeat the opposing team by dribbling by everyone. When I encounter a player like that, I have rarely been able to improve that individual's game. Everyone can learn but it is a lifelong process.

For me personally, I learned the most about "getting better one mistake at a time" from my mother. She married young, never had education beyond high school and came to

Canada as a young woman, with almost no knowledge of the English language. I recall her telling me the story of her first Thanksgiving, where she did not realize the amount of time it took to cook a massive frozen turkey. She was one of the first Chinese wives allowed to accompany her husband to Canada. To her chagrin, a group of bachelor students who were invited over for the meal had to chip in and cook the turkey to salvage the evening. It was a humiliating experience that obviously stayed with her.

My mother, though, had a tough spirit. She always said to me, "Let me show you the right way to do this." She was rarely wrong. However, she taught me that everything she learned was through an examination of her mistakes. Whether it was cooking, learning how to do her taxes or sewing, she looked at every single task, corrected every error and made a conscious decision that she was going to improve her approach to improve her efficiency and the resulting product. She hammered this into me as a child and the lessons resonated with me throughout my life. I now subconsciously do this in everything I do. When I had to help remove and tear out the interior of a house for ten hours, what motivated me to continue was the drive to constantly improve my efficiency. If I had to remove the frame around a window, I challenged myself to find a better way to do the next one. I turned this mundane task into one where I could continue to challenge and improve myself.

Although to others my mother may have appeared to be a tiny Asian woman who wasn't even 5' tall, to me she was a giant who could accomplish far beyond her education and her language limitations. She ended up being one of the top income tax consultants for H&R Block, was renowned throughout the Chinese community for her cooking ability, and her ability as a seamstress was legendary. She taught me that if you are willing to learn from your mistakes and constantly improve, the sky is the limit. In fact, the only limit that is reached is when you decide that you are done pushing the envelope of your capabilities. When you think you have reached perfection, then that will be your last and most serious mistake.

6. Pain is Weakness Leaving the Body

In this chapter, I cover my second coaching mantra. "Pain is weakness leaving the body" is what I repeat to my players as we are doing strength and core training. I believe this is from the U.S. Marines and reputedly said by General Lewis B. Puller. I love the saying as it illustrates a concept that so many young people lack: work hard till it hurts.

Getting into university presumably is difficult as it is reserved for the best and most capable individuals. Now, with the high failure rates in university, one fact is becoming obvious. If it were easy to get through the undergraduate program to get that degree, everyone would be doing it. Obviously, not everyone is capable and one factor that determines who will and who won't make it through is work ethic.

There is much talk these days about the 10,000 hour rule. This is a principle that was brought into the public consciousness by Malcolm Gladwell in his book *Outliers* where he points out that many that we consider to be prodigies actually have spent 10,000 hours of dedicated practice to hone their craft (Gladwell, Outliers: The story of Success, 2008). These include the Beatles, who spent four years daily toiling in Hamburg night clubs. This grueling experience allowed them to become the incredible phenomenon they were when they hit the Ed Sullivan show in 1964. What is remarkable about that performance is that it happened without modern amplification and monitors. In other words, with all the girls screaming, the band was actually not able to hear each other and had to rely on these hours of practice to pull off their legendary performance. Other examples include Bill Gates, who spent hours a day programming to reach that magical 10,000 hours. There is much virtue in hard work that will pay off in the end.

As mentioned in Chapter 3, hard work is one of the things that professors are not seeing in their first year students. The reason for this is that, if work ethic is not something learned at early age, it is exceedingly difficult to grasp the concept when you hit university. The National Survey of Student Engagement (NSSE) indicated in 2004 that only 10% of students were fully engaged in their studies. There were 40% who were partially engaged and would do less than what is expected. This leaves 50% of the students who are disengaged with school and are doing very little work in their studies (Cote & Allahar, 2007). Recall that I mentioned that the top 10% of the students are as good as they have ever been. I suspect that this set of students overlap significantly with the fully engaged students in the NSSE study. This is actually good news in that, all you need to do is to get into that top group and you will ultimately succeed. One way to do this is to develop a great work ethic.

In this chapter, I will be drawing on the similarities between developing a good work ethic and doing a physical workout. Now, one of the hardest things when starting a workout regimen is to keep it going. It must become a habit. In many ways, the tools one would use when trying to push yourself when exercising can be used to help develop self-discipline in your studies.

One of the most important aids in staying with a fitness program is finding good workout partners or even a trainer to work with. I know this has always been the case for me. For school, this translates into finding people who, like you, want to work on their self-discipline and work ethic. If you are with a group of people who only want to party and hit the bars, you will find it very difficult to put in the hours you will need to be successful. If your university has an office with resources to help you develop self-discipline, engage them as soon as possible. Like a personal trainer, getting a professional to work with you, to give you valuable advice and to keep you accountable can be a critical difference-maker.

One thing that often deters the novice athlete is that they want immediate results. Every January, gyms are full of people who have made New Year's resolutions to lose weight. Sales of exercise equipment skyrocket just before Christmas, mainly from those with delusions of having a fit body by the following summer. Usually by mid-February, the lineups in the gym are long gone and the classified ads are full of almost new exercise equipment for sale. What causes these individuals to give up is that they were focusing exclusively on an ambitious final goal and, when they didn't hit their goal in a short period of time, they gave up. Thus, when developing self-discipline in school, it is important to break down the final goal into small steps. Just like the overweight person who needs to concentrate on losing a few pounds at a time, you need to break down your attempts to improve your work ethic into workable small steps. Take the total amount of time that you can realistically work hard at one sitting and try to increase it slightly. Try your hardest to meet this new target. If you fail, simply adjust and try again. If, however, you try to suddenly double the amount of time you sit and study at one time, you are setting yourself up for failure.

One thing that surprises the players that do my core and strength training is that, when one starts with a realistic goal and gradually increase their performance, one can actually improve quite rapidly. Players who can barely do 30 seconds of a plank but start doing what they can, continue to work at it consistently and gradually add a few extra seconds every week, soon find themselves, in a few short weeks, exceeding their initial modest target and hitting 60 seconds. Those who are bent on getting the 30 seconds right away at the start basically never even hit that minimal target because they end up failing and quitting.

It is also important to try to work on a fixed schedule. My workout routine starts typically at 6am, when the kids are still in bed and I am not distracted. For years now, I am up almost every day to do my exercise regimen. It has now become a habit. Similarly, you need to set up a schedule of time periods when you are determined to sit down and work. Try to determine what time of day that you are most productive. Some people are morning people and some are evening people. Don't fight your own nature but find the time periods when you work best. Do not let anything interfere with those times. As you progress, constantly monitor when and how long you have these work periods. Just like an athlete, however, as you find it easier to work the scheduled periods, start to stretch them out a little longer every week. A novice long distance runner may start out doing 2 miles but every week, they can add a bit more. Soon, they are doing 5 miles with minimal strain. In a similar way, once you get into a routine, you can start to increase the length of time you can maintain at a sitting doing schoolwork.

Where you do your work is almost as important as how long you work. Some people need dead silence to work. Others don't mind having music playing. Some like the comfort of their home whereas some need to be in an academic environment. It is curious that there have been studies that indicate students who prepare for an exam by practicing on a previous exam tend to do better if they write the previous exam in a classroom that resembles where they will write the actual exam (Nist-Olejnik & Holschuh, 2011). You need to find this optimal study location for yourself.

One trick to help you maintain long study periods is to give yourself regular little breaks throughout. It is possible some people have the ability to work 10 straight hours on school work without a break, but I am not one of those. Try to take regular short breaks. You may want to take a ten minute break every ninety minutes. You should also take a significant break in the middle of an especially long session. You will find that this will give your brain a bit of a rest and that you will be more productive in the end.

Finally, break the course work into two types of tasks. There will be some, like memorizing or working through some difficult concepts, that will need a great deal of intense concentration. There will be others, like creating a spreadsheet, doing the simpler questions on an assignment or rewriting the day's notes to make them legible, that take far less mental focus. Try switching between these tasks for a break. In other words, when you are done memorizing some important facts, rather than abandoning studying to give yourself a break, do one of the less strenuous mundane tasks to relax yourself. In this way, you are still doing something important to the course but are not burning yourself out.

At the end of the day, you are shooting for an upper limit. Just like the marathon runner doesn't need to train for more than 23 miles, similarly, you only have a limited number of hours you can possibly shoot for. In Chapter 3, we spoke about the 2 hours for every hour of lecture minimum. At crunch time, this might extend to 3 hours. Assuming 15 hours of lectures, you should be aiming for around 45 hours per week with a few weeks perhaps peaking at 60 (note that these include the lecture times). These peak weeks should only happen once or twice a term though. If these look like crazy hours, keep in mind that, at a full time job after graduation, you will be putting in similar hours. Look at this exercise as helping to develop the level of work ethic you will need for future employment. This is often what differentiates those with successful careers from those who stall in their career advancement. It just makes good sense to develop those qualities that will carry you far later in life.

The queen of hard work is my beautiful wife, Jodie. She entered medical school at age 17 and I believe she is the hardest working medical student that the University of Saskatchewan has ever seen. At graduation, Jodie knew exactly how many hours she spent studying every topic and it far exceeded the 60 hours per week maximum that I advocate. She had a gift of being able to focus and work for incredible stretches at a time. This drive allowed her to forge not only a successful career as a physician but has also gave her the drive to home-school all nine of our children. Whenever someone feels that I am trying to give students unreasonable goals, I simply point out the archetype of hard work, my wife.

Once you begin to improve your work ethic, you should see immediate results. It turns out, however, that this is just the first step. As pointed out next chapter, work ethic and self-discipline aren't the only factors contributing to academic success. However, it is an excellent starting point.

7. Develop Grit

An exciting new concept that was introduced in 2007 is that of grit. Grit is defined as perseverance and passion for long term goals. This is the personality trait of working hard toward a goal and not giving up, even when faced with failure and lack of apparent progress (Duckworth, Peterson, Matthews, & Kelly, 2007). Sound like first year? If it does, perhaps it is time to try to develop this important characteristic for success.

In Duckworth's seminal research, grit was found to be more important than self-control and conscientiousness in achieving success. To be successful requires years of persistent practice with very long-term objectives. A person with grit does not change from task to task. People with grit will actually try to set themselves up for potential failure in order to ultimately master their craft. In my opinion, based on the struggles we are seeing with present day students, grit has been decreasing in the general student population. Thus, when students hit their first obstacles, the initial inclination for these students is to just give up. However, if students in the past had this desirable characteristic and could overcome these stumbling blocks, then it must be possible for us to retool the education system to help current students to find grit.

There are well developed grit test questionnaires. There are several variations but the below is an example[1]. In the test, one relates how closely the statements match the student.

1.   New ideas and projects sometimes distract me from previous ones.
2.   Setbacks don't discourage me.
3.   I have been obsessed with a certain idea or project for a short time but later lost interest.
4.   I am a hard worker.
5.   I often set a goal but later choose to pursue a different one.
6.   I have difficulty maintaining my focus on projects that take more than a few months to complete.
7.   I finish whatever I begin.
8.   I am diligent.

Points 1, 3,5 and 6 are related to low grit whereas the others are strong indicators of high grit. The studies by Duckworth et al compared the results of these grit tests to student success in various scenarios (Duckworth, Peterson, Matthews, & Kelly, 2007). One study looked at an online survey comparing grit with completion of secondary and post-secondary degrees. This study demonstrated that grit was related to the completion of higher academic degrees

---

[1] https://sasupenn.qualtrics.com/SE/?SID=SV_06f6QSOS2pZW9qR

(eg. those that completed a Ph.D. were grittier than those who had only an undergraduate degree). Grit also increased with age although the authors speculated that, for cultural and social reasons, grit may be decreasing through the generations (which is my suspicion as well). A second study was conducted with undergraduate psychology majors, comparing SAT scores as well as grit to GPA. The study showed that grittier students were more successful in GPA than their peers, despite having lower SAT scores. Another study involving the prestigious West Point Military Academy showed that grit was able to predict boot camp retention far better than any other factor, including SAT. A final study examined the relationship between grit and success in the National Spelling Bee. As expected, those with higher grit tended to go further in the competition.

This research has attracted significant recent attention. The U.S. Department of Education, for example, is planning to devote enormous resources into the impact of grit on the education of students (Office of Educational Technology, Feb, 2013). This will require a new look at the priorities given in secondary school to certain topics. For example, the first victims of any belt-tightening in high school curriculum are often physical education and music programs. However, in both these subject areas, one is given tasks where the expectation is initial failure (e.g. playing a new piece of music or trying a new sport). With hard work, the student is expected to gain confidence and joy from overcoming their initial deficit and succeeding. I believe strongly that these subject areas can strengthen a student's grit. In fact, when I choose graduate students, I will often give the edge to those candidates who have a strong background in athletics or music. I am very rarely disappointed by these students. Yet, I constantly hear from parents how courses in these important subject areas are being cut in their local high school. Grit studies indicate that this is the worst possible decision.

In a very interesting study by Warren Willingham, a sample of 4814 students who were entering a selection of ten private colleges were studied (Willingham, 1985). The focus was on the 3676 who graduated from fourth year. It turned out that the most effective indicator of academic success from their application information was having a multi-year commitment to an extracurricular activity. The results were even better for those who excelled at these activities. This is further evidence that grit, although it was not called that in those studies, is a contributing factor to academic success.

One very important factor for a person to have grit is to have passion for the subject. Now, if you are struggling, it may be difficult to try to forget about your present predicament and reflect back on why you had wanted to be in your current area of study. If things were going well, is this subject area really what you want to do for the rest of your life? If the answer is yes, then try to put aside your current struggles and focus on the fact that this is truly your passion. This is a crucial first step. If you are in a program because of pressure from your parents, just wanting to be in a subject area with your friends or because you think the money will be good at the end, then you may be fighting a losing battle. You need genuine zeal in order to ignite the passion for academic success.

The second aspect of grit is perseverance for long term goals. This is of course related to the previous three chapters in that, if you can learn from your mistakes, display good work ethic and put your setbacks into perspective, then you are partway there in terms of getting grittier. In fact, I have seen how this aspect of grit has impacted my own children in their education. All nine of my kids are all heavily involved in sports. Most of them were below average in both work ethic and skill level in sports when they were young but, for some of them, shortly around the age of ten, a switch went on in their head where they began to understand the role of working hard in their sports. They went from playing recreational to high level sports in their teens. One won a national championship in Ringette and several won or were finalists in provincial level competitions in hockey and soccer. What I found very interesting is that, as they began to increase their effort and excel in sports, they had a similar improvement in their academics. They went from being average students to near the top of their class, even once they entered university. There seems to be something about being able to persevere and work hard that seems to be transferable, at least in my kids, to academic success.

To demonstrate grit, there are some fairly simple concepts that you must continue to reinforce in yourself. First, you need to keep going when you have reached the limits of where you think your abilities lie. Whereas most people quit at that point, you must find it within yourself to continue onward. For example, when doing a problem set, push yourself with the harder problems. The ability to repeatedly take challenging problems and force yourself to improve is referred to as deliberate practice (Duckworth, Kirby, Tsukayama, Berstein, & Ericsson, 2010). Instead of spending time going over the easier problems, those who have grit tend to spend more hours repeatedly working on the hardest questions. Using a sports analogy, to become a good basketball player, one cannot practice dribbling without working on the hard moves that takes a long time to master.

It isn't sufficient to keep pushing yourself, however, if you are hitting a brick wall each time. In order to keep progressing each time, you must find a way to give yourself immediate feedback (Duckworth, Peterson, Matthews, & Kelly, 2007). If you are a struggling student, this means that you will need to focus on deliberate practice but with continual feedback at all times. This may mean creating a study group where you work together on problems and help each other. It could means seeking out teaching assistants or professors to get help. If you don't have continuous access to your instructors, consider hiring a tutor on a weekly or biweekly basis in order to get quick feedback. Even though this is an expense, it is much less expensive than failing out of university.

Developing grit is, in many ways, similar to running a marathon. I really like this analogy for the following reason.

When a person runs in a marathon, there is a point close to the twenty mile mark where the runner actually has used up all the glycogen in their blood, which is one of the main sources of fuel stored in their body. Marathon runners refer to this as "hitting the wall" and there are numerous stories of runners who just stop running because their body is essentially shutting down. In other words, this isn't just a psychological barrier but also a physical one. To overcome this, a good marathon runner needs to beat this barrier with mental toughness. One tool that is used is to create a positive mantra that one repeats, where all the words focus on the positive. An example is to keep repeating to oneself, "I just need to finish this next assignment, hand it in and then I will be in very good shape" or "I just need to finish studying one more section for the final exam and I will be in a good spot to do well on the exam". Once you have completed this task, however, immediately create a new achievable milestone and repeat the mantra. You are essentially breaking down a huge task that may cause you to "hit the wall" into smaller steps that are more manageable. Like the runner that just focuses on running to the next lamp-post, one can take positive feedback from accomplishing all the small milestones and eventually, the major goal is accomplished.

Another tactic that marathon runners do to keep going is to use visualization techniques. Try to imagine in your mind passing the next exam and the resulting feeling of relief and satisfaction. Keep focusing on that picture. Don't forget to give yourself a little reward when you do succeed.

Another tool to try to persevere and become grittier is to keep thinking of alternate schemes to improve your results each time you repeat a task. Challenge yourself to improve with each repetition. If you are doing a laboratory with repetitious procedures, keep thinking of ways to improve your efficiency. Try to think outside the box when coming up with solutions. As I mentioned, this is a trait that has been hammered into me from a young age by my mother. Even now, I still find myself looking for the "best way to do a task." Finally, analyze how those students who are ahead of you are strategizing to succeed, and try to adapt their techniques to your own approaches.

One huge deterrent from becoming a gritty individual is that some people have difficulty starting a task. In other words, they procrastinate. It can be very difficult to get things started. My suggestion is to just jump in, realizing that you will make mistakes. As a professor, I see many students who are literally frozen into inaction. If it helps, you can start with a few easier tasks, keeping in mind that this has to translate into deliberate practice with harder tasks very quickly.

Another barrier for becoming gritty is your mindset. Carol Dweck has done research into what she labels as fixed mindsets versus growth mindsets (Dweck, 2006). Those individuals with a fixed mindset go into a task feeling that their abilities and/or their intelligence is fixed and unchangeable. Thus, any outcome, such as passing or failing an exam, becomes a validation or even a judgement of who they are as a person. If they pass, they are "smart" and if they fail, they are "stupid". Those students with a fixed mindset do well as long as they are always in the former state. However, they fear doing poorly and, if they fail, they automatically label themselves.

Those with a growth mindset, on the other hand, believe that abilities and intelligence are malleable. They believe they can continue to learn and improve. Thus, they do not label themselves as either a success or a failure based on any one outcome. In fact, a setback is merely feedback in their learning. They see value in the effort. Regardless of whether a growth mindset individual has had a good or bad outcome, they treat everything as a learning experience.

Fixed and growth mindsets were shown to be a predictor of student success in a study conducted with a large pool of grade 7 students (Dweck, 2006). Tests were given to determine whether students had a fixed or growth mindset. The study showed that, when facing academic failure, fixed mindset students would study less whereas growth mindset students would study more. In general, the marks of the fixed mindset students fell but the growth mindset students had the opposite trend. A study of pre-med students taking chemistry courses showed similar trends. Those with growth mindsets bounced back but the fixed mindset students would let setbacks adversely affect their academics.

As a student, you need to ask yourself which mindset you have. If you are not sure, ask yourself this simple question. When you don't do well, do you examine yourself to see what you did wrong so you can learn from it or do you tend to see a setback as demonstrating that you are incapable of doing well?

The good news is that Dweck claims that growth mindset can be taught. Even learning that there are two types of mindsets can affect your ability to change from a fixed to a growth mindset (Dweck, 2006). It is also helpful to imitate how growth mindset students learn. Fixed mindset students often looked to memorize. They study for the test to try to get that good mark. Growth mindset students will look at key concepts in order to understand a subject. They are constantly looking at their mistakes to try to improve. They are studying to learn and not just to regurgitate the material at exam time.

One other way to influence yourself is to be careful that you are not inadvertently labelling yourself when evaluating your academic results. Dweck points out an interesting phenomenon about positive labels. When students encounter hard problems and are told that they did well because they are smart or talented, it inadvertently pushes them into a fixed mindset. If they don't do well the next time, they begin to believe that they are not smart or talented. If, instead, it is the effort that is praised, it seems to lead the students to a growth mindset, and they will tend to continue to improve academically (Dweck, 2006). So, when you start turning the corner and doing better in school, be careful not to tell yourself that you are smart for doing well.

Instead, focus on the effort you exerted to get to this point and take pride in that. Regardless of how you are doing academically, focus on the effort, not the results, since this is the only thing you have control over. Eventually, this should help you shift into a growth mindset. You must continually monitor yourself. Mindsets do not change overnight so one must be patient.

An important aspect of grit is that you must be seeking constant feedback in order to keep improving. If you have no one to get feedback from, then you need to be brutally honest with yourself. It is the only way for you to develop a growth mindset and grit. When the opportunity arises, ask someone else to evaluate you without sugar-coating the results. Frank feedback is important. Make sure you aren't asking your parents or your best friend to assess your work. As a music columnist for fifteen years, I was constantly sent music by artists who were convinced that they were God's gift to the entertainment industry. When I rejected their recording, they would retort by stating that their family and friends told them they were extremely talented. On the other hand, I have song-writing colleagues who are incredibly frank and will reject any material from me that they feel is weak. Without this input, there would be no way that I could be successful as my initial attempts to be creative are often pretty abysmal. It is incredibly valuable to get honest feedback. This is something that every student should seek.

As you start to develop a growth mindset and become a grittier individual, keep challenging yourself with tougher problems. Keep seeking feedback. Remember to praise the effort and not the result. If you fail, tell yourself that you don't get it yet but you will if you continue the effort. Finally, I am sure that the concept of becoming a grittier person and changing your mindset seems very daunting. However, remember that just knowing about mindsets can impact your ability to foster a growth mindset. Combining this with the previous three chapters should give you the tools to become a grittier individual. One lesson that I carry throughout life is that anything worth doing will be hard. If that were not the case, then everyone would be doing it.

8. Reinvent Yourself

As you go through this book, "change yourself" is a common theme that runs through everything. That is the only thing you actually have control over. Your teachers, your classmates, your exams and all these other external factors may have contributed to your problems but focussing on things that you cannot change will not help your situation. You may be wondering, however, if it is at all possible to change and reinvent yourself. I am going to relate to you a couple of stories to help you understand that it is possible to change. In my case, it is truly possible to teach an old dog new tricks.

As mentioned, I have had a bit of success in the Christian music industry. As a child, I had always been interested in music, but more as a spectator. I loved music so much that I started doing concert promotion and organized a few major music festivals. I began to rekindle my interest in singing at the age of 27. I auditioned for a local theatre group and starting to sing in church. Definitely, no one at that time would have thought that I had any future in music. However, at the age of 35, I decided to form, with a few friends, a band to introduce youth to contemporary Christian music. The band was called Critical Mass and, working with some fabulous songwriters, we released a demo recording that ended up selling a couple of thousand copies. I even tried my hand at song-writing and was a co-writer of a few songs on the album.

The band received enough notoriety that we decided to do a professional recording. I worked hard at song-writing and, with lots of brutal critiques from my bandmates, made an even bigger contribution on the new album. We released the album "Completely" when I was 38, and the album ended up winning Best Rock Album honours at the Canadian Gospel Music Association in 2000. With this album gaining critical success, I decided to use my promotion and marketing skills to try to get one of the biggest gigs ever.

Pope John Paul II was coming to Toronto in 2002 for World Youth Day and I sent probably a dozen press kits for my band to anyone I thought was even remotely connected to the booking end of this event. To make a long story short, at the age of 40, I got to sing and perform in Toronto for a crowd of almost a million people (see **Figure 3**).

Figure 3

At this point, most of the band members of Critical Mass decided to pursue other interests (how do you top a live performance with that many people?) but I still wanted to record. So, at the age of 43, I set about to record a concept album where I was going to contribute to virtually every song on the album. In 2005, this album, entitled "Grasping for Hope in the Darkness", won Best Rock Album honours again at the Canadian Gospel Music Association awards.

The moral of the story is simple. If an Asian university professor can start, at the age of 35, a music career that has garnered major music awards and an audience of a million people, then you surely can change yourself to succeed academically. The secret to my success was dogged determination and never really accepting that there were limits to what I could accomplish. In short, I demonstrated grit. I had to learn how to sing, song-write and manage a band at an age when most people would have thought that it would be naïve to gain any sort of success.

Now, you could claim that this really didn't involve a change in personality, which is what we are asking for when we are talking about changing a mindset. Although this is difficult, it is not impossible, as I am about to share.

At one point, in all the busyness of all my activities, I began to neglect my family. The pressure got to me and I began to be a parent that I was not proud to be. I got ill-tempered and was really unpleasant to be around. It got so bad that I was faced with one of the most catastrophic moments in my life. My wife and I separated for a time.

I once had a friend who committed suicide after his separation. I could understand what he went through. The potential of losing your family is one that penetrates to the depth of one's heart. I had to make a change but it truly did involve re-examining who I was as a person and what kind of husband and father that I truly wanted to be.

I am happy to say that my family and I have reconciled. However, I had to change virtually everything about my parenting. I also had to look deep within myself and try to change the root cause of my issues: my self-centeredness. It was a tough battle and is one that is still ongoing. I knew I had to make a change in my personality or else I was going to lose my family. You may be in a situation right now where you need to make a change in YOUR personality in order to salvage your education. If I can do it, then so can you. You need to be determined that this is absolutely necessary to achieve academic success.

When my wife and I were struggling in our marriage, we attended Retrouvaille, which was an excellent program for marriages that are on rocky ground. One of the biggest lessons we learned was that feelings are neither right nor wrong, they just are. Love, on the other hand, was not a feeling but a decision. In other words, one had to choose to love and to work on a relationship, regardless of how you are feeling. You needed to acknowledge your feelings but then decide to move forward. Similarly, in your current situation, you may be feeling frustrated, angry, anxious, depressed, sad or desperate. What you need to do is to realize that these feelings are there but then decide to move on and to keep going. Your academic success should not be defined by your feelings but by a conscious decision to become a gritty student who will be successfully academically.

9. Strategize to Win the Game

This chapter is one where you will receive some very practical advice on how to improve your potential for academic success. We will start by looking at more general strategies and then drill down to very specific tools to use in your academics.

9.1 General Strategies

Before delving into very practical ways to improve your academic abilities, you may need to rethink the motivations behind why you are in university.

9.1.1 Attitude toward Learning

One of the first things you need to do is to change your attitude toward learning. As a professor, I am constantly asked the question "Why do I need to learn this?" Keep in mind that a lot of what we are teaching you may not be something that you will need specifically in your day to day duties in your future job. Many students will decide that, because a topic is not "useful", they will put only a half – hearted effort into learning the material.

As a student, you must understand that we are not just teaching the specific topics in the course syllabus but we are also teaching you how to think. You may not use a particular idea you see in a lecture but the concepts may be useful elsewhere. Consider a complex theorem and the associated proof in mathematics. You may never see or use this proof ever again. However, the methods used to prove the theorem teaches you a rigor that you may need elsewhere in your courses or even in your future career. You can't anticipate what you will need to know in the future. For example, many engineers work for financial institutions after graduation because their mathematical way of thinking appeals to employers in this sector. They may never use the engineering principles that they learned but those pesky math courses that seemed so irrelevant are now helping to bring in a pretty generous salary.

If you approach your schooling with the attitude that you want to learn for learning's sake, it will be become much easier to motivate yourself. It is almost certainly the case that a lack of motivation will affect how you do in a course in a detrimental fashion.

Although this may seem obvious, many students need to be reminded that education is not just about being entertained. It always surprises me to see how many students' motivation to work hard in a class is based on how amiable and lively the professor is. Don't get caught in this trap. Don't be a student who blows up his academic career just because some of his instructors are "boring" and "uninspiring".

9.1.2 Deep Learning

Another key mistake made by students is to study just for the sake of doing well on the test. They only care about what will be on the exam and try to learn so that they will know the answers for the test. The goal of every student should be deep learning. Deep learning means that the student is focused not just on details but on being able to take the knowledge, understand it and then integrate it and apply it to new exciting scenarios outside of what is taught in the classroom (Pellegrino & Hilton, 2013). To help the student focus on deep learning, I would like to point out that, in my experience, a student's future success does not depend on whether a student has an A average. It will depend on his job experience and ability to be innovative. It would be much better in the long run to be a deep learner with an 80 average than a rote-memorizer with a 90 average.

You might also hear educators refer to other similar concepts. You may encounter the idea of students either motivated by mastery goals or performance goals. Mastery goals are similar to the concept of deep learning in that there is a desire to attain a true understanding of a subject area. Performance goals are those where the objective is just to do well on the test or assignment (Ames & Archer, 1988). The terms extrinsic versus intrinsic learning is also sometimes encountered. Extrinsic learners are motivated by external outcomes (eg. getting a good job, receiving praise) but intrinsic learners are motivated by the enjoyment of learning

(Ryan & Deci, 2000). At the end of the day, the goal of every student should be to take the deep learning strategies from their university studies to become life-long learners.

A simple trick to see if you have deeply learned a topic is to see if you can explain it to another individual. Try to give a quick mini-lecture to another student. Einstein is claimed to have said that if you cannot explain a concept to a six year old, you truly don't understand it yourself. This is a great way to test whether you have truly been a deep learner.

9.2 Specific Strategies

The general strategies discussed above are the new framework through which to focus on the particular practices to achieve academic success.

9.2.1 Fundamentals

Many students have a critical weakness in their poor understanding of the fundamentals. As pointed out in Chapter 3, regardless of what they are taking in university, every student needs to have a working knowledge of basic English and Math. Even in engineering and the sciences, there is an enormous amount of time spent in documenting results. If you are struggling in these areas, you need to get tutors to help you as soon as possible. Many universities have resources to help in this respect as well.

If you have to submit documents for evaluation while your English skills are still shaky, consider proofreading services. There are many options available online to help you at a very reasonable rate.   In the meantime, the best way to improve is to practice. Use every opportunity to write. Try to become an avid reader.   Don't be afraid to take your written documents and get them critiqued by a friend or by a teaching assistant.

9.2.2 Learning Styles

Everyone learns in different ways and you will need to figure out what kind of learner you are. In education theory, there are all sorts of categories that researchers create in order to describe different types of learners.   In my opinion, the most relevant to classroom learning is the VARK model; Visual, Aural, Reading/writing and Kinesthetic (Fleming, 1995).   Again, these may not conform to other expert opinions. Depending on the book or paper, all sorts of other learners are described in the literature but these are the most relevant to my discussion.

Visual learners like using pictures and figures to help them understand material. They will often learn better from powerpoint presentations. If this sounds like you, try to study keeping this in mind. For example, as you go through your notes, you may want to make figures (e.g. a mind map, block diagram or flow chart) to help tie concepts together. One of my daughters is very much this type of learner.

When she was taking a course on biology, she would make very complex diagrams from her notes to help her understand, for example, the evolution of plants (see **Figure 4**). They were literally works of art but it greatly aided her studying.

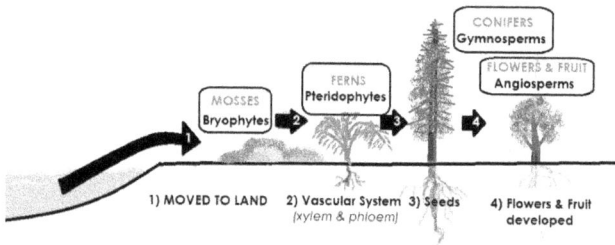

Figure 4

Aural learners find that they gain more information by listening than by reading. Lectures are very helpful as they can listen attentively to the instructor. They will make up mnemonic devices or little songs to help them remember material. If you are in this category of learner, try to study by using these types of tools. For example, it might be helpful, with the instructor's approval, to record lectures and play them back.

Reading/Writing learners, on the other hand, prefer to learn by reading and writing information down. They will highlight their textbooks or summarize notes on paper to help cement concepts into their mind. These learners often have an advantage because so much of current instruction relies on reading and writing to convey information.

The most disadvantaged students are kinesthetic, who are those who learn best by touching and manipulating objects. Classrooms are rarely set up to help these learners unfortunately. Still, for some subjects, it may be helpful to try to build little physical models to aid in learning. A chemistry student may, for example, build molecules out of styrofoam balls and toothpicks to help them in their understanding. A student might want also to give a mock lecture on a topic, using lots of body and hand motions to help cement the ideas into his brain. For myself, when trying to memorize the dozen pages of lyrics that go into putting on a live concert, I find that choreographing the performance in my head helps me to memorize all the words, since phrases are now associated with an actual physical action.

Few students are exclusively in one of these categories. In fact, depending on the subject, they may shift to a different type of learner. Some may be a combination of categories. Learners who are both visual and aural may, for example, find going to YouTube to find online video tutorials to be helpful. Nonetheless, it is important, when studying, to understand how your mind best processes information and to play to your strengths.

It is also important to attempt to learn in other learning styles which are not your strength. Often in life, you have no choice as you will only be presented one learning paradigm. You need to pick up competent skills in all these learning modalities. No lecturer has the time or ability to cater their content delivery specifically to every type of learning style.

9.2.3 Learn To Be a Serious Student

One of the biggest mistakes that students make is to skip lectures and tutorials, particularly if they find the lecture dry. It takes a great deal of discipline to force oneself to go but I believe it is very important. Often, lecturers will give important information about the class (due dates, lab updates or even exam hints) which you don't want to miss. In tutorials, ask the teaching assistant lots of questions. It is a great time to get some feedback on your understanding of the course. It also never hurts to hear the material presented in class, even if the delivery of the content is suboptimal.

It is good practice as well to prepare before coming to a lecture. Try to spend 15-30 minutes going over the previous lecture the night before. If you are a visual learner, add some figures or diagrams to reinforce the ideas. An aural learner may want to read through the notes again aloud. If you are a linguistic learner, take a few minutes to summarize the notes. If you have time, look forward a bit to check out the topics in the new lecture. You will be amazed at how much time you end up saving by staying on top of the course material.

My advice, as well, is to always sit near the front of the class. It is much easier to be engaged. As well, the professor tends to remember those in the front few rows and that may come in handy when you need help or if your mark is just on the borderline. Sometimes, being a recognizable name or face can be invaluable. If you are near the front and still have trouble understanding the professor or reading his handwriting because he goes too fast, ask the professor if you can record the lecture or if you can photograph the board to help keep up. You can always ask for handouts from the professor as well. If you don't ask, the answer will certainly be no. Try to be proactive rather than reactive.

It may be helpful to work with a friend to make sure your notes are complete and things weren't written down in error. Resist the temptation to take turns going to lectures. That isn't the point. As well, don't try to write down every word the professor says. Learn to summarize and capture key points. Never be afraid to ask the professor questions if he is going too fast. You can be pretty confident that you won't be the only person who is lost.

Finally, it is critical that you learn how to pay attention. You must turn off the laptop and don't send text messages on your phone. Contrary to what you may think, you cannot be on Facebook and focus on the lecture. I have even witnessed students playing computer games on their laptops! There have been numerous studies that show that not only your marks will go down but so will the marks of all those around you who are distracted by your actions (Oliveira, 2013).

9.2.4 Learn how to Read

Unfortunately, in high school, students are not taught how to read effectively; especially, how to read textbooks or papers. Many students try to go from line to line, trying to absorb the material in a linear fashion. What I suggest to students is to read things differently. It is better to go from what I call the 10,000 foot view and then drill down into the details. Practically speaking, it means that if you are reading a chapter in the textbook, start by reading the introduction and the conclusion section to get an overview of the material being taught. Then, look at the sections and skim through to see what the general ideas are for each section. After you have done this, you will find that it is easier to read from line to line as you now have a picture of the entire chapter. This is a useful tactic if you have been asked to read a paper. Check out the abstract, introduction and conclusion before starting to read the paper. As well, don't be afraid to write notes in your textbook. You probably can't sell it on the used market after marking it up but your education is worth the sacrifice!

9.2.5 Learn how to Write

Many students do not have the ability to write. Papers that are handed in to me are rife with spelling and grammatical errors. This age of texting and tweeting has also led to students who cannot seem to communicate in entire sentences. Often, papers read as if the student had sat down at his laptop and started typing whatever popped into his head.

You must learn how to communicate your ideas clearly. It is absolutely critical to write an outline. Jot down the main points that you want to get across, organize these points and then fill out each of these points with further ideas in point form. Start to formulate chapters and sections using only point form. Make sure you have an introduction and conclusion. Create an extended outline where each section is broken down in point form. Only then should you begin to write. Remember that each chapter, section and paragraph should start with an introduction, the main points of the argument and then a concluding statement. After you do this, proofread carefully or ask a friend to help proofread. If English is not your first language, you can search for proofreading services on the Internet.

As you start to research your paper, you might find that you don't even know where to start looking. My suggestion is to go to the library to get help from the librarians. They are paid to help you figure out where to look for your background research. When you find some related books or papers for your topic, then use the bibliography to help you find more papers that were written previously. You can also use the Internet to do a citation search, which finds other papers that have used the papers you have found as a basis for their work. In this way, you can work backwards and forwards in time to find more and more papers for your paper.

As you do your background research by reading books and papers, make sure that you make notes about everything you see. Don't rely on your memory. I have seen many students read several books and paper, but, when it came time to write the document, they could no longer remember what they read. When you make notes, it is better to paraphrase rather than use the wording from your source. There will be little chance of plagiarism if you make your notes in this way.

As a student, take every opportunity to write. This is a skill that will be useful everywhere in life. In fact, the more interesting the job, the more likely it will be that you will need to communicate your ideas in a coherent manner. Writing will give you an invaluable skill for life.

9.2.5 Learn how to Speak

Some people feel that the ability to communicate verbally is something that should come naturally. On the contrary, good orators are very hard to find. Many jobs rely on the ability to deliver a presentation in a succinct manner.

Unfortunately, there are few opportunities in high school to gain this experience, outside of the occasional memorized soliloquy in English class or the drama club. University offers fewer opportunities still and it is easy for students to avoid the experience of standing in front of an audience, battling nerves and answering potentially challenging questions. Sometimes it is a case that English is not the student's first language. Sometimes, it is the fear of losing self-esteem. Regardless, I encourage students to take advantage of any opportunity to deliver a verbal presentation.

My father is a prime example of someone who struggled initially with public speaking. He came from China and had an accent. Yet, as a professor, he was called upon to speak in front of the classroom every week. He used his accent for humor and learned how to speak slowly and clearly. With sustained practice, my father improved to the point where all his students were able to understand his lectures despite his difficulties in English. In fact, he was one of the most highly regarded lecturers in his department.

The ability to speak also applies to communicating in a professional manner in the classroom. Think carefully and choose your moments to ask questions in class. It is just as futile to ask questions geared to impress the professor as it is to ask questions every time you have the slightest confusion. Don't hesitate, however, to ask questions of the professor or the teaching assistant after class. When doing so, make sure you have a list of coherent questions and make sure you have tried the textbook or your peers first before going to them for help. Ask the teaching assistant before asking the professor. Many professors have limited availability whereas the teaching assistant is being paid to be the first point of contact for questions regarding the course material.

9.2.6 Exam Preparation

Unfortunately, one of the only ways that professors can evaluate students is through the dreaded examination. This is a very artificial way to test knowledge as many students cram for the exam. However, if we were to ask the students a few months later to try similar questions to what was on the exam, most students would find that they could not recall anything but the simplest details. That being said, exams are a necessary evil and here are a few tips on how to do better.

First, you need to see from the course syllabus what sections will be on the exam. By attending lectures, you can get a feel for what type of a professor you are dealing with. Is he into the details or is he a professor who looks at subjects from a high level? Likely, the tests will reflect this. The quizzes and midterms are also a good way to understand what the final exam will really be like.

When preparing for the exam, take a look at an old exam or ask previous students who have been taught by this professor what kind of questions are likely to be asked. Ask the professor if he could distribute an old exam. Most professors would be happy to do so. When you study, keep in mind the type of questions that may be asked. As you read through old exams, see if you can picture similar questions from your course notes and textbooks that could be formulated.

If the exams tend to be multiple choice, search the Internet to see if there are sample exams covering the same subject area that you can try. Again, look through the types of questions and, as you are studying your notes, try to formulate similar sample questions.

At some point, you want to try to write some of these old exams for practice. When you do this, simulate the environment that you will be writing in. Try studying and writing the practice exam in the same or a similar classroom to where you will be actually writing. There is some evidence that indicates your ability to recall is directly connected to where you learned the material (Unsworth, Spillers, & Brewer, 2012).

When writing the exam, never start from the first question and work through the questions in sequence. Always have a glance through the exam. See how much each question is worth. Tackle the easier questions with more marks assigned first. Build your confidence. Often, the hardest questions on the equation are not worth a huge amount of marks but are placed there to help the professor separate the A students from the B students. Yet, if you spend on your time on the hard question, you could be missing out on some easy marks.

When you are answering a question, be neat and organized. Put in as much explanation as possible. When a student just puts down an answer with minimal detail, there are very few part marks that the professor can give to the student. If you are running out of time, try explaining to the professor how you would answer the question. This can sometimes result in a few part marks. Don't try for volume however. I have seen students spend a great deal of time writing a lengthy tome (and wasting time) but getting a zero. Finally, don't forget to at least make a guess on the multiple choice questions that you have not done. They may gain you a few more marks.

9.2.7 Time Management

In Chapter 3, one of the biggest hurdles in first year was time management, according to the students (Bentein, Frenay, Verwaerde, Bourgeois, & Galand, 2003). I would concur based on what I see from my students. My first suggestion is for students to create a daily planner, preferably using an electronic one. Go through your course syllabus to see what the various deliverables are in order to create a task list with deadlines attached. As soon as the professor assigns work, update your planner. Estimate how much time it would take to do each assignment, project or other task, and make sure you create sufficient blocks of time to do the work. It is better to base your planning on a worse-case scenario rather than an optimistic time span. Try to space out the work and start early so that, if you run into any difficulties, you have an opportunity to re-plan. For every day, remember to plan in time to do preparatory reading for each lecture as well as time at the end of the day to review that day's notes. For major projects, create milestones that are realistic and moderately ambitious. For example, set a date when you will accomplish all the reading, another for creating an outline, one for an extended outline, then one for writing and a last one for proofreading. Try to work consistently towards these milestones. Keep yourself accountable by not letting milestones slip or you will find yourself on a slippery slope. Do all you can to meet these milestones and reward yourself when you do. As you as you complete these milestones, create new deadlines immediately. If you miss a deadline for reasons beyond your control, don't beat yourself up over it but just re-plan immediately. Finally, do not forget to plan to have large blocks of time preparing for midterms or finals.

I mentioned earlier in the book that you need to spend at least 2 hours of studying for every hour of lecture. Although this gives the minimum time that one should spend on average on a course, you will need to prioritize exactly what work to do within this 45 to 60 hour window each week. Take a look at what work are worth the most marks and focus in particular on those deliverables. For example, I have seen students spend 90% of their time in a course on assignments that are only worth 10% of the final mark, while at the same time, they neglect studying for the final exam which is worth 50% of the overall marks. You don't necessarily have to give equal time to all parts of the course.

There is also the idea of diminishing returns. To produce an essay that gets a mark of 90% takes time but it is not simply 10% more effort to get to 100%. In some cases, one needs to double the amount of time to achieve perfection and, even then, so much depends on the marker. If you have finite time, balance how "perfect" you will aim for. If it is a project worth 30% of your final mark, you can spend more time aiming for those extra marks, but if the deliverable is worth only 5%, then this time would be better spent on other activities.

In a course, not all topics are equal. There will be certain topics that the instructors will consider to be the threshold concepts. These are key concepts that are critical to the subject area and are necessary to continue to understand and build on the knowledge in that area. An example would be, in high school physics, the idea of a free body diagram or conservation of energy. A student needs to be able to identify these concepts and then focus more energy on these concepts.

I find that many students who are struggling academically are also struggling with procrastination. When faced with a large exam or a large project, they make any excuse to not do the work. My advice is to really force yourself to take that first step. Study just one section, write just a paragraph or just do one assignment question to get started. The first step is the most important and the hardest. Don't get frozen into inaction.

9.2.8 Group Work

Group work is actually something that many of us have to deal with on a daily basis in our careers. However, for many students, university is their first taste of having to work with other individuals. This can be exceedingly difficult. For some, it is an opportunity to ride on someone else's coat tails. As you can imagine, this is something I do not recommend. Frustration can also occur when your group members don't pull their weight. If you are doing a lot of work and there are slackers in the group, my suggestion is to take the high road and keep working hard. That being said, document your meetings and all your interactions so that, should the opportunity arise and there are severe problems, you will have evidence that you can present to your professor. Keep in mind that uneven workload in groups is a real reflection of what you will encounter in real life. To make things worse, you will likely find in your career that those who can get things done are given even more to do. My suggestion is to wear this as a badge as opposed to weighing yourself down with frustration.

For major projects, you and your group members should break the project into smaller tangible subtasks. You need to divide the subtasks up between the group members and make a group member accountable for each subtask. This doesn't necessarily mean that the person in charge of a subtask has to do all the work. He can ask for help at any time but he is ultimately responsible for ensuring the subtask is done on time. In this way, you can maximize your chances of completing the project with minimal complications.

As I mentioned previously, it is very important who you choose to work with. One suggestion is not just to work with your friends, although it may seem comfortable and easier to do so. Try to get together a group where there are a variety of skills. There could be some members who are more details oriented and some that are higher level thinkers. Some may write very well and some could be good at organizing content. An effective group will have skill sets that complement each other. As well, by seeking out different group members, you will get to know other people and extend your network of contacts.

Projects are often where one really needs to keep track of diminishing returns. When you are in the middle of an intense deliverable, you can easily forget how much the project is worth in the overall scheme of things. Make sure you are aiming for great but not perfect.

9.3 Cheating

When students are starting to sink, there is a temptation to get through the obstacle by cheating. This is simply not the answer. First, you will be surprised at how easily professors and TAs can spot suspicious documents. As well, there is more software available now that can be used to detect plagiarism. It is not worth it and, even if you get away with it in the near term, you will eventually be in the work place where you will not be able to continue the cheating behaviour without catastrophic consequences.

10. Time is on Your Side

It is alarming that the median completion time for an undergraduate degree is now six years with 60% taking at least this long (Cote & Allahar, 2007). This is not a good statistic and is far larger than the nominal four years. It is good to know, however, that, if it looks like your academic troubles are going to cost you some time, that you are not the only one in this boat. At some point, you may be asked to take a break before coming back. You may need to repeat some of your courses. Don't look at this as an end to your dreams but as an opportunity to come back with a renewed commitment to academic success.   At your young age, it may seem like an unmitigated disaster but, trust me, looking back through the lens of age, even a delay of a year or two is not a big deal. The important thing is to succeed in getting your academic degree.

As an employer or as a potential graduate degree supervisor, you should know that evaluators are often looking for trends. In fact, between two applicants, if one has a steady B average and one has worked their way steadily from a D to a B average, employers will often take the second candidate, simply because of the fact that they are willing to gamble that the upward trend will continue.

If you are struggling academically, you should not strive for the difficult goal of getting immediately back to your high school average.   Start with realistic goals and push your marks a bit higher every academic term.   In this way, you are not pushing yourself into unrealistic expectations which may cause you to despair and give up. Many of my most successful graduate students have taken this path. In almost all these cases, I was rewarded by having these students continue to improve academically throughout their graduate degree. One of the best students I have ever had the privilege of supervising actually failed out and had to leave university for a time. The extra maturity and determination that he displayed coming back into the program served him extremely well. He ended up finishing his Masters degree twice as fast as any other typical student.

We are also looking after university for deep learners, not just those with marks. Now, marks might get you into your first job but after that, employers no longer look at your transcripts. You may find this hard to believe but when you are applying for your jobs, your university marks matter far less than what you have accomplished in your previous job position. It is true that without a university degree, it is exceedingly difficult to get a job but beyond that, having an A average isn't really going to help you that much. Employers realize that individuals who understand a subject area deeply and can apply the material to different problems are much more useful than those who studied just to get good marks. Employers don't want people who just regurgitate knowledge but what those who seek to go beyond just the facts. They want individuals that not only know how things work but also understand the underlying principles to make things work even better.

11. Keeping Balanced

Maintaining a balanced lifestyle may seem like an impossible task but there are numerous reasons why a student should try to strive for this. It is important so that the stress doesn't get to you. Balance can help put all your current troubles into perspective. It can also be very important after you graduate. If you can't keep a balanced lifestyle in university, it will be highly improbable that you will be able to after you get out of the academic environment and into the workplace.

First, if you are still looking into universities to attend, don't necessarily get sucked into the "ivy league or bust" mindset. There are advantages to going to a university that is close to home. You can save tuition and living expenses, for example. As well, contrary to popular opinion, a degree matters and but it is less important where you got it. Malcolm Gladwell points out in his book, *David and Goliath: Underdogs, Misfits and the Art of Battling Giants*, that it is actually better to be a big fish in a little sea than vice versa (Gladwell, 2013). In other words, being a good student in a smaller university rather than an average student at more prestigious university leads to more success after university.

If you are staying on campus residence and find it difficult to study because of all the partying, then you need to find a place off campus. That being said, you need to make sure that you can still connect socially with others. As well, there are cost savings if you share a place off campus and learn to cook for yourself rather than eating expensive and often unhealthy residence food.

Saving money becomes very critical as, at some point, many students who cannot manage a budget end up having to get a job. It is better to graduate with some debt than to get a job to support yourself through university. A loan is better than spending 15-40 hours working and trying to keep on top of your studies. In the long run, this makes better economic sense as well, since, failing out means you have essentially wasted all the money that you spent on tuition and living expenses.

In a study of Belgian university students, a shockingly high 1/3 of all students stated that they felt lonely in university (Bentein, Frenay, Verwaerde, Bourgeois, & Galand, 2003). This is very ironic since university is a place where cliques cease to exist. This should be the ideal place to make new friends, where even the jocks and the nerds can all put aside their differences and co-exist. However, I often see students who seem to cling to their high school memories and friends. When they struggle in university, it seems they want to withdraw into that world again but everyone has already moved on. Students need to disconnect from their past and move forward. The same issue applies to family connections. Some students spend every weekend travelling home to the comfort of mom, dad and siblings. This is an easy trap to fall into when you are struggling. Of course, you should always reach out when you need to talk to someone, but when it causes you to withdraw from the university environment, you could be on the path to failure.

One also needs to develop a social network in school. You should consciously plan specific times and lengths of time where you can meet with friends, make new friends and take a break from the grind of academic life. Be strict with yourself and when the socializing time is up, plan to leave and return to your studies. Under no circumstances allow your social calendar to encroach upon your 45 (or 60 as a peak) hours per week of school work. Another reason to allow yourself the luxury of socializing is to create a network of contacts. When you have graduated, you will find that having a large network of people that you know will help you immensely in your career. In fact, the most successful students after graduation tend to have averages that range from the high-70s to mid-80s, but who are well balanced individuals that have a great network of contacts.

I cannot emphasize enough that students need to find balance in a healthy lifestyle. Do your best to eat healthy, sleep well and exercise. You don't want to fall victim to the Freshman 15 (ie the number of pounds a freshman gains on average). Not only will you find it difficult to lose the weight, it is also a fact that a healthy body does indeed lead to a healthy mind. By taking regular exercise breaks (even taking a long walk is good), you will be amazed at how much clearer your mind becomes and how much more productive you are. You should also try to get at least a half hour of vigorous exercise every day. If you can develop this habit in university, you will also find it easier to continue once you get into the pressures of a family and job.

Once you have stabilized your academics, you may want to consider joining a club or some other group on campus. In this way, you can start to develop some hobbies. At university, you will have access to numerous free or nearly free activities. You can try a sport that you have always wanted to try. Ballroom dancing, drama, music, debating or anything you can dream of trying are possible activities. Too many students never explore these opportunities. Besides giving you a mental health break, you never know when the skills you pick up in a hobby might come back to help you. In my life, my ability to perform on stage has helped me immensely in lecturing. When one is a performer, one learns to block their performances or, in other words, plan where you will move and stand at any given time in a song. It is quite a skill but a necessary one. Seeing a great singer standing totally stationary, regardless of how good they are, is akin to staring at a boring picture for an hour. No movement is extremely boring. Even a bit of movement from time to time gives the audience a visual break. Watch a concert next time and see how a skilled performer works the stage. When I lecture, essentially, I am actually working a stage in my head. I try to be animated but also to move around from time to time to keep the students engaged. Another example of a hobby helping in real life is coaching soccer. When you coach a team, you are really gaining huge expertise in how to get a group of diverse individuals working together toward a common cause. Everyone has their strengths and weaknesses. The coach's job is to assign duties and exercises to help everyone improve and to help the team be successful. This was invaluable when it came time for me to start up my technology company, Handshake Interactive Technologies Inc.. The team included technical and non-technical expertise. Some people were high level thinkers while others were very detail-oriented. In this way, the team had a diverse skill set that allowed us to succeed. Without my interest in soccer, I may not have been as successful in starting up my business.

The last area of your life where you need balance is in the spiritual realm. If you don't take care of your spiritual well-being, you may find yourself despairing more easily. Now, for some of you, this may involve getting re-involved with your church, mosque or synagogue but what if you are an agnostic or atheist? The same principle applies. If you don't have a particular religious background, you can still have spiritual balance by reaching out into your community and helping others who are not so fortunate. Work at a homeless shelter, food bank or be a big brother. This is very important because having spiritual balance can help put all your troubles into perspective. You may have failed a midterm but there is a family out there struggling to eat. You may have had to pull a few all-nighters but you aren't struggling with an addiction that threatens to marginalize and kill you. By taking a few hours each week or even month to do something spiritual, you will find it much easier to bounce back after your own failures. As an example, psychologist Adam Grant studied a University of Michigan Fundraising call centre (Dominus, 2013). A student who benefitted from the funds spoke to the people working at the call centre and told the story of how his life was impacted. The net effect of realizing their work had an impact on others caused the call centre workers to double the funds they were able to solicit. The conclusion is that knowing we are benefitting others motivates us to work harder. So, in a very real way, spiritual balance can actually help you academically.

I want to emphasize that one needs balance but don't swing too far in the non-academic direction. Make sure these activities happen after your scheduled school work. In this way, you can always be certain that you are tending to the needs of both social/spiritual and academic.

Finally, if you do find things spinning out of control even if you have sought spiritual balance, then seek help right away. Every university has resources to help manage stress and depression. It is vital to recognize when you can't seem to rejuvenate yourself after talking to friends, family or advisors. Don't wait too long before taking action. The other advantage to seeking help is that the resources at the university can be an advocate for you, should you need intervention with a stubborn or uncaring professor. They can document your troubles and help you find a resolution with your professors, including getting you potentially more time for exams.

12 Concluding Remarks

I hope that, whatever brought you to this book, that you will find some of the suggestions useful. You may be going through a very difficult time right now but it is also a time that is ripe with opportunity, if you can overcome your current struggles.

I mentioned at the start of the book that many of the issues faced by students are from external causes that are outside their control. You may feel as if life and your education is spinning out of control. Hopefully, by reading this book, it can cause you to reflect and to begin to get yourself out of this downward spiral.

You may want to check out some other books that will help you in your drive to become a better student. The following are all books that go into far more detail, as my goal was to make this book short and readily accessible.

Much of the description of the current crisis in education was drawn from *Ivory Tower Blues: A University System in Crisis* (Cote & Allahar, 2007). This is an excellent book that describes the huge disconnect between high schools and universities. It also gives much more context to how these problems came to be and what needs to be done to address these issues.

To help you get over the despair of your current academic predicament, there is an excellent book entitled "Sometimes You Win, Sometimes You Learn" (Maxwell, 2013). I highly recommend you grab this as a resource to help you put your mistakes and problems in perspective. The book is full of inspiring stories of individuals who have faced what you are going through but have succeeded beyond your wildest dreams. Best of all, it is written in a highly entertaining manner and I am sure you will find it very enjoyable.

A book that is often used to inspire students to stop focussing primarily on marks is *What the Best College Students Do* (Bain, 2012). The author illustrates, using many examples and interviews with students and professors, why students need to focus on deep learning and not merely on marks. He demonstrates that, after all is said and done, those who are successful did not need high marks; they just needed to learn deeply from their undergraduate degree.

In terms of more practical advice on study habits and how to become a better student, the book *College Rules!* (Nist-Olejnik & Holschuh, 2011) goes into far more detailed strategies for achieving academic success. It is a great book that expands on the ideas espoused in Chapter 9. I highly recommend that book as a follow up to this one.

A large section of the book was devoted to the concept of grit and mindset. Outside of the papers mentioned in this book, there is an excellent book entitled *How Children Succeed: Grit, Curiosity, and the Hidden Power of Character* (Tough, 2013) that covers numerous other examples of grit at work in helping students become successful. If you are interested in the growth versus fixed mindset, the book, *Mindset: The New*

Psychology of Success (Dweck, 2006), is very readable. Not all the chapters are applicable to students but the earlier chapters in the book are very helpful.

Now, for some of my readers, you may have tried everything in this book and the others, but nothing works. Well, if that is the case, there is no shame in trying hard and not succeeding. I can guarantee you that the education that you did receive made you a more well-rounded person. I can also tell you that there is no dishonour in pursuing a trade or some other honest living. Some of the smartest people I know are ones that can build, fix, clean or maintain. Some of the most frustratingly incompetent people I know have doctoral degrees and make me want to give up on the human race. There is no connection to your position in life and how much you will impact the world.

In closing, in my career, I have seen many students work themselves out of situations where things looked pretty bleak. I hope that you will be one of the successful ones and, if this book helped even in the slightest in pushing your academic career forward, then the time I spent working on writing this was well spent.

Bibliography

ACT. (2013). ACT National Curriculum Survey: Policy implications on Preparing for Higher Standards. *ACT.*

Ames, C., & Archer, J. (1988). Achievement Goals in the Classroom: Student's Learning Strategies and Motivation Processes. *Journal of Educational Psychology,* vol. 80, no. 3, 260-267.

Bain, K. (2012). *What the best college students do.* Harvard University Press.

Baumeister, R. (2005, Winter). Rethinking Self-Esteem- why nonprofits should stop pushing self-esteem and start endorsing self-control. *Stanford Social Innovative Review.*

Bentein, K., Frenay, M., Verwaerde, A., Bourgeois, E., & Galand, B. (2003). Understanding academic failure among the first entrance university students for promoting academic achievement. *Poster presented at the Biennial Conference of the European Association for Research on Learning and Instruction.* Padova, Italy.

Boesveld, S. (2013, Feb 2). In praise of failure: The key ingredient to children's success, experts say, is not success. *National Post.*

Canadian Sports Centres. (2005). Canadian Sport for Life: Long-Term Athlete Development Resource Paper.

Carlson, K. B. (2012, Sept 12). No winners: Children still keeping score despite move to end sports competition. *National Post*.

Collins, N. (2011, Oct 14). Video games can alter children's brains. *Telegraph*.

Cote, J., & Allahar, A. L. (2007). *Ivory Tower Blues: A University System in Crisis*. University of Waterloo Press.

Crocker, J., & Park, L. (2004). The Costly pursuit of Self-Esteem. *Psychological Bulletin*, Vol. 130, no. 3.

CTV News. (2009, Sept 2009). Students not prepared for university, says survey. *The Canadian Press*.

Dominus, S. (2013, March 27). Is Giving the Secret to Getting Ahead? *New York Times*.

Duckworth, A. L., Peterson, C., Matthews, M. D., & Kelly, D. R. (2007). Grit: Perseverance and passion for long term goals. *Journal of Personality and Social Psychology*, Vol. 92, no. 6, 1087-1101.

Duckworth, A., Kirby, T., Tsukayama, E., Berstein, H., & Ericsson, K. (2010). Deliberate practice spells success: Why grittier competitors triumph at the National Spelling Bee. *Social Psychological and Personality Science*, vol 2, pg 174-181.

Dweck, C. (2006). *Mindset: The new psychology of success*. Random House LLC.

Ferguson, S. (2005, June 6). How computers make our kids stupid. *Macleans*.

Fleming, N. (1995). I'm different; not dumb- Modes of presentation (V.A.R.K.) in the tertiary classroom. *Research and Development in Higher Education, Proceedings of the 1995 Annual Conference of the Higher Education and Research Development Society of Australasia*, Vol 18, 308-313.

Friday, T. (2010, June 1). Win a soccer game by more than five points and you lose, Ottawa league says. *National Post*.

Gladwell, M. (2008). *Outliers: The story of Success*. Penguin UK.

Gladwell, M. (2013). *David and Goliath: Underdogs, Misfits and the Art of Battling Giants*. Little, Brown and Company.

Goodman, M. (2012, Feb 13). Are we raising a generation of helpless kids? *Huffington Post*.

Griesemer, N. (2013, May 1). ACT Report says high school students are not prepared for college. *Examiner*.

Jerema, C. (2010, July 8). Your Grades Will Drop. *Macleans*.

Matthews, A. (2001, Aug 20). Computer games children anti-social. *Telegraph*.

Maxwell, J. C. (2013). *Sometimes You Win- Sometimes You Learn.* Center Street.

McMahon, T. (2011, Nov 16). Parents cry foul after elementary school bans balls over playground safety. *National Post.*

Moore, H. (2014, Feb 25). Cheating students punished by the 1000s but many more go undetected. *CBC News.*

Nist-Olejnik, S., & Holschuh, J. (2011). *College Rules! How to study, survive and succeed in college.* Random House LLC.

O'Connor, J. (2012, May 1). When there are no winners in sports, everybody loses. *National Post.*

Office of Educational Technology. (Feb, 2013). *Promoting Grit, Tenacity and Perseverance (Draft).* U.S. Department of Education.

Oliveira, M. (2013, August 14). Student's use of laptops in class lower grades: Canadian Study. *The Globe and Mail.*

Pellegrino, J., & Hilton, M. (2013). *Education for life and work; Developing transferable knowledge and skills in the 21st century.* National Academies Press.

Rigoglioso, M. (2005, August 24). High Schools Fail to Prepare Kids. *Stanford Report.*

Rushowy, K. (2009, April 6). Profs blast lazy first-year students. *Education Reporter.*

Ryan, R., & Deci, E. (2000). Intrinsic and Extrinsic Motivations: Classic Definitions and New Directions. *Contemporary Educational Psychology*, Vol. 25, 54-67.

Schwartz, Z. (2013, March 29). High-School grade inflation balloon ready to pop. *Globe and Mail.*

Steinberg, L., Brown, B. B., & Dornbusch, S. M. (1997). *Beyond the Classroom.* Simon and Schuster.

Tamburri, R. (2012, January 18). Are High School Marks Enough. *University Affaris.*

Tough, P. (2013). *How Children Succeed: Grit, Curiosity and the Hidden Power of Character.* Mariner Books.

Unsworth, N., Spillers, G., & Brewer, G. (2012). Dynamics of context-dependent recall: An examination of internal and external context change. *Journal of Memory and Language.*

Willingham, W. (1985). *Success in College: The role of personal qualities and academic ability.* New York, NY: The College Board Publications.

www.ingramcontent.com/pod-product-compliance
Lightning Source LLC
Chambersburg PA
CBHW071455070426
42452CB00040B/1364